A NEW SPECIAL RELATIONSHIP

FREE TRADE AND U.S. - CANADA ECONOMIC RELATIONS IN THE 1990s

BY PETER MORICI

Centre for Trade Policy and Law

The Centre for Trade Policy and Law (CTPL), established in 1989, is jointly sponsored by The Norman Paterson School of International Affairs at Carleton University and the Faculty of Law at the University of Ottawa. CTPL was established to promote greater public understanding of trade policy issues, to foster independent analysis and research of trade policy issues, and to encourage the development of trade policy professionals. The core of the Centre's program includes a range of interrelated activities:

Teaching. Starting with increased resources dedicated to teaching graduate and professional students at the two sponsoring universities and programs for government staff and business and labour organizations, CTPL will act as a catalyst to the development of teaching programs at other Canadian universities by working with faculty in sponsoring the preparation of teaching materials, encouraging faculty interchanges and holding periodic seminars on the teaching of trade policy in Canada.

Seminars and Conferences aimed at wider audiences where academics, government officials and private sector specialists can explore a range of trade policy issues and stimulate greater public discussion of trade policy issues.

Research and Publications. CTPL encourages both applied and theoretical research in the area of trade policy by helping qualified scholars obtain the necessary funds to carry out their research. Research will also be promoted through the publication of refereed monographs and conference proceedings as well as the development of a resource centre to act as a central repository for material on trade policy. CTPL will promote its national mandate by inviting scholars from across Canada to participate in seminars, special lectureships, conferences and research projects and stimulate a flow of human resources between academic, government, business and labour organizations.

The Institute for Research on Public Policy

A National Presence

Founded in 1972, the Institute for Research on Public Policy is an independent, national, non-profit organization with offices across Canada.

The mission of the Institute is to improve public policy in Canada by promoting and contributing to a policy process that is more broadly based, informed and effective.

In pursuit of this mission, the Institute:

- identifies significant public policy questions that will confront Canada in the longer term future, and undertakes independent research into those questions;

- promotes wide dissemination of key results from its own and other research activities;

- encourages non-partisan discussion and criticism of public policy issues in a manner which elicits broad participation from all sectors and regions of Canadian society, and links research with processes of social learning and policy formation.

Method of Operation

The Institute is decentralized, employing researchers across Canada. This ensures that research undertaken by the Institute involves contributions from all regions. The Institute also works with individual researchers or institutes in other countries.

Independence and Neutrality

The Institute's independence is assured by an endowment fund, to which federal and provincial governments and the private sector have contributed.

A New Special Relationship

Free Trade and U.S.-Canada Economic Relations in the 1990s

WITHDRAWN

A New Special Relationship

Free Trade and U.S.-Canada Economic Relations in the 1990s

by

Peter Morici

Centre for Trade Policy and Law
and
The Institute for Research on Public Policy
L'Institut de recherches politiques

Printed in Canada

Legal Deposit Third Quarter
Bibliothèque nationale du Québec

Canadian Cataloguing in Publication Data

Morici, Peter.

A new special relationship

Prefatory material in English and French.

ISBN 0-88645-132-9

1. Canada—Foreign economic relations—United
States.   2. United States—Foreign economic
relations—Canada.   3. Canada—Economic policy.
4. United States—Economic policy.   I. Centre for
Trade Policy and Law.   II. Institute for Research on
Public Policy.   III. Title.

HF1480.15.U65M67   1991   337.71073   C91-097675-9

Camera-ready copy and publication management by
PDS Research Publishing Services Ltd.
P.O. Box 3296
Halifax, Nova Scotia B3J 3H7
(902) 494-3865

Published by
The Centre for Trade Policy and Law
Room 204, Social Sciences Research Building
Carleton University
Ottawa, Ontario K1S 5B6
and
The Institute for Research on Public Policy
P.O. Box 3670 South
Halifax, Nova Scotia B3J 3K6

Contents

List of Tables

Foreword

Implementation of the Canada-United States Free Trade Agreement (FTA) on January 1, 1989, may have dampened somewhat the Canadian debate over the agreement's overall merits. But continuing Canadian concerns about economic relations with the United States and U.S. preoccupations with global economic challenges signal the need for a greater understanding of the specific implications of the FTA for the management of the bilateral relationship. This subject assumed particular interest as an economic downturn began to take hold in both countries immediately following signing of the agreement, forcing industry to adjust more quickly to new competitive realities. In a broader context, because of lack of agreement to date on key issues during the current Uruguay Round of GATT negotiations, bilateral or regional trade agreements have attracted greater attention as options for trade policy. Questions have also surfaced about the impact of the FTA on the actions of private firms and governments alike in responding to the challenges of global competition. These issues gained further importance and relevance with the initiative by the United States and Mexico, subsequently joined by Canada, with respect to a trilateral North American Free Trade Agreement.

In this study, Professor Morici examines from an American perspective the impact of the FTA on the evolution of the Canada-United States economic relationship. First, his analysis puts into historical context the "special" trading relationship between Canada and the United States which prevailed over the early postwar period. Forged during the crisis of the Great Depression and the exigencies of World War II, that special diplomatic relationship between the two federal governments disappeared as a wider array of governmental and private actors impinged on the bilateral relationship. Second, Morici examines how FTA rules and dispute settlement procedures create an effective basis for managing bilateral economic relationships in the context of these more decentralized policy processes. Third, he explores the potential impact on the bilateral trading regime of the changing nature of international competition, the adjustments taking place in the structure of the Canadian and American economies, and the challenges posed by continuing technological change. Given the impact of these factors, Morici argues that the FTA's usefulness in managing bilateral trading relations should be judged in terms of how effectively the two national governments can use the agreement to manage their commercial relationship in the context of global competition and their broader multilateral policy goals.

Of particular interest are Professor Morici's comments on how the United States may respond to declining competitiveness. He notes two developments in the 1980s that may have significant implications for United States trade policy: the greater receptivity by American industry to joint ventures with competitors; and the emergence of a more active industrial policy. With respect to the latter, Morici argues that under President Reagan, one saw the beginnings of a shift in industrial policy from mere support for mission oriented research, which assumes a viable industrial base, to programs that actively seek to assure the maintenance and expansion of that viable industrial base. This focus on precompetitive research was accentuated by the acknowledgement of the potentially massive leverage of an effectively-focused program of defence spending. While he argues that the United States under President Bush has retreated somewhat from an activist industrial policy, the implication for Canada is that American industrial policy could well attract R & D activities and innovative manufacturing from Canada to the United States, with evident repercussions on the bilateral relationship.

Professor Morici completes his analysis with an insightful discussion of the implications of regionalism for countries within and outside regional blocs. In his view, a North American Free Trade arrangement including Canada, the United States and Mexico is consistent with the evolving structure of global competition and the effective management of economic relations between trading partners.

The Centre and the Institute are pleased to publish jointly this important contribution to better understanding of the evolving nature of the Canada-United States economic relationship and Canada's stake in it.

Murray G. Smith
Director
Centre for Trade Policy and
 Law

Rod Dobell
President
Institute for Research on Public
 Policy

July 1991

Avant-propos

La mise en application de l'Accord de libre-échange entre le Canada et les États-Unis, le 1er janvier 1989, a peut-être quelque peu refroidi le débat canadien sur les mérites de l'accord dans son ensemble, mais les Canadiens continuent pourtant à s'inquiéter des relations économiques avec les États-Unis, et les Américains sont toujours absorbés par les défis économiques globaux. Cela indique clairement qu'il faut absolument en arriver à une meilleure compréhension des implications spécifiques de l'Accord pour assurer la bonne gestion des relations bilatérales. Cette question est devenue peu à peu évidente lorsque la crise économique a commencé à se faire sentir dans les deux pays, tout de suite après la signature de l'entente, forçant l'industrie à s'ajuster plus rapidement que prévu aux nouvelles réalités de la concurrence. Dans un contexte plus vaste, du fait que les négociations de l'Uruguay Round du GATT ne soient toujours pas parvenues à résoudre certaines questions-clés, les ententes commerciales bilatérales ou régionales ont commencé à être sérieusement envisagées comme d'autres options de politique commerciale. On a également commencé à se poser des questions relativement à l'impact de l'Accord de libre-échange sur les actions des firmes privées tout comme des gouvernements, en réponse aux défis de la concurrence globale. Ces questions ont pris encore davantage d'importance et de pertinence à la suite de l'initiative prise par les États-Unis et le Mexique, à laquelle le Canada s'est joint par la suite, en ce qui concerne l'Accord de libre-échange nord-américain trilatéral.

Dans la présente étude, le professeur Morici examine, d'un point de vue américain, les effets de l'Accord de libre-échange sur l'évolution des relations économiques entre le Canada et les États-Unis. Pour commencer, il présente la situation historique des relations commerciales «spéciales» qui existaient entre le Canada et les États-Unis pendant les premières années de l'après-guerre. Élaborées pendant la crise de la Grande Dépression et compte tenu des exigences de la Seconde Guerre mondiale, ces relations diplomatiques très particulières entre les deux gouvernements fédéraux disparurent dès que toute une ribambelle d'intervenants gouvernementaux et privés mirent le pied dans ces relations bilatérales. Ensuite, M. Morici examine de quelle manière la réglementation de l'Accord de libre-échange et les procédures de règlement des différends constituent une base efficace pour la gestion des relations économiques bilatérales, dans le contexte de ces processus politiques plus décentralisés. Enfin, il explore l'effet possible de la nature changeante de la concurrence internationale sur le régime de commerce bilatéral, les ajustements qui s'opèrent dans la structure des économies canadienne et américaine, et les défis posés par les changements technologiques continus. Étant donné l'impact de ces éléments, l'utilité de l'Accord de libre-échange pour la gestion des relations commerciales bilatérales devrait être jugée selon l'efficacité avec laquelle les deux gouvernements nationaux réussissent à se servir de l'entente pour gérer leurs relations commerciales, dans le contexte de la concurrence globale et de leurs objectifs de politique multilatérale de plus grande envergure, selon M. Morici.

Les commentaires de M. Morici sur la manière dont les États-Unis risquent de répondre à l'affaiblissement de la concurrence sont particulièrement intéressants. Il cite deux développements des années 1980 qui risquent d'avoir des effets importants sur la politique commerciale des États-Unis : le fait que les industries américaines se sont montrées plus réceptives à la création de compagnies mixtes avec des compagnies concurrentes, et l'émergence d'une politique industrielle plus active. En ce qui concerne ce dernier développement, M. Morici pense que, pendant la présidence de Monsieur Reagan, on a pu constater les débuts du changement qui s'est opéré dans la politique industrielle. De simple soutien pour la recherche orientée vers une mission particulière, ce qui suppose l'existence d'une base industrielle viable, celle-ci est passée à la mise sur pied de programmes qui cherchent activement à assurer le maintient et l'expansion de cette base industrielle viable. Cette nouvelle importance accordée à la recherche concurrentielle s'est accentuée lorsque la force potentiellement extraordinaire d'un programme de dépenses défensif bien ciblé a été reconnue. Bien que M. Morici soit d'avis que la politique industrielle activiste des États-Unis ait quelque peu régressé sous la présidence de Monsieur Bush, la politique industrielle américaine pourrait fort bien attirer les activités de recherche et de développement et la fabrication innovatrice du Canada vers les États-Unis, et ceci aurait des répercussions évidentes sur les relations bilatérales.

Le professeur Morici complète son analyse par une discussion bien informée sur les implications du régionalisme pour les pays situés à l'intérieur et à l'extérieur de blocs régionaux. Selon lui, une entente de libre-échange nord-américaine entre le Canada, les États-Unis et le Mexique cadre parfaitement avec la structure changeante de la concurrence globale et la bonne gestion des relations économiques entre partenaires commerciaux.

Le Centre et l'Institut sont heureux de publier conjointement cette contribution importante qui devrait permettre de mieux faire comprendre la nature en pleine évolution des relations économiques entre le Canada et les États-Unis, et ses implications pour le Canada.

Murray G. Smith
Directeur
Centre de droit et de
    politique commerciale

Rod Dobell
Président
Institut de recherches politiques

Juillet 1991

Acknowledgements

I wish to express my thanks for the kind support of the Business Fund for Canadian Studies in the United States, the Canadian Embassy in Washington and the Institute for Research on Public Policy.

Many people had a hand in helping me shape my ideas. Most noteworthy among these were Murray G. Smith and Michael Hart who commented on the manuscript. Many others commented on portions of the manuscript and provided ideas as well.

My thanks go also to Frank Wihbey, Head of Government Documents at the University of Maine Library; my research assistants, Denise Gamba, John Schneider and Michael Jonason; my typist, Gail Fernald; and the staff of the Canadian Embassy Library in Washington. I retain responsibility for the contents and any errors.

Peter Morici
University of Maine

Introduction

The 1988 federal election was cast as a seminal decision about Canada's future. The ruling Progressive Conservative Party and its supporters argued that the Canada-U.S. Free Trade Agreement (FTA) would secure the nation's economic future. FTA's detractors charged the agreement would not deliver promised benefits, especially long sought shelter from American protectionism. Canadian nationalists characterized the election as a contest for Canada's soul. They argued, whatever the benefits, the FTA would endanger Canada's distinctive identity, compromise its social programs and foster political integration with the giant to the south.

As is often the case, electoral rhetoric on both sides overstated reality. The FTA must be understood in the context of factors influencing economic relations between the United States and Canada. The FTA goes a long way towards providing Canada with more secure access to the U.S. market, but many issues were left to follow-on negotiations.

By eliminating tariffs and reducing other impediments to trade and investment, the FTA will encourage more bilateral commerce and industrial specialization. But fast growing markets in Asia and Europe and prospects for declining U.S. current account deficits in the 1990s make it unlikely that the U.S. share of Canadian exports will exceed pre-FTA levels.[1] Certainly, pressures will persist for Canada to harmonize economic policies with the United States, but these emanate from other international developments. Among the latter are the much heralded globalization of markets and enterprises and the further integration and extension of the European Community (EC), which challenge Canada to achieve access to broader markets.

Beyond the specific commitments and goals embodied in the agreement, the FTA re-establishes the special relationship that had characterized the conduct of U.S.-Canadian relations during World War II and through the 1950s. As the United States adjusts and crafts policies in response to its altered competitive position, the FTA provides the framework to shelter or at least buffer Canada from the adverse effects of these actions.

Ultimately, Canada's decision to enter into the FTA should be assessed by its contribution to its ability to cope with changing global realities in the context of its asymmetrical relationship with the United States and its broader goals for national unity.

The Promise and the Challenge

The FTA represents both a promise and a challenge.

Embracing virtually all aspects of bilateral economic relations, the agreement commits Canada and the United States to establishing a more open, predictable and secure environment for bilateral commerce. At its core, the agreement constitutes a political commitment to reduce the influence of unilateral actions on bilateral commerce, to rely more on jointly-articulated rules for defining and enforcing the rights and protections afforded each country by General Agreement on Tariffs and Trade (GATT) principles, and to broaden, deepen and more precisely articulate the scope of these rights and protections as they apply in the bilateral context.

Yet, the FTA is not a done deal. The scope and complexity of problems discussed in less than 20 months of negotiations required that broad goals be set for issues such as subsidies, product standards and services with the expectation that specific compromises could be hammered out later. As such, the agreement aims for a process of progressive liberalization as much as it creates a free trade area. The pace of progress in continuing negotiations will importantly affect the success of the FTA, but such progress is far from guaranteed.

During the 1980s, the FTA emerged from fundamental changes in the international economic environment and distinctive Canadian and American reactions to them. Maintaining the momentum towards more open markets could prove difficult as the challenges and opportunities posed by the international economy change. For example, the globalization of enterprises and accompanying transoceanic exchange of capital, technology and corporate control could provoke conflicting U.S. and Canadian responses. More aggressive U.S. industrial policies could engender bilateral frictions. Similarly, a bilateral, Mexico-U.S. free trade agreement could reduce both the benefits Canadians receive from the FTA and support in Canada for further liberalization under the FTA. Hence, Canada has joined the trade talks with Mexico.

Moreover, the FTA adds to the adjustment pressures already being imposed on North American industries by global shifts in comparative advantages, technological change and resource depletion. These forces increasingly pit U.S. and Canadian communities against one another in competition for plants and jobs. Regional and sectoral pressures for subsidies and protection remain strong and will likely persist as sources of bilateral tension.

In the end, the issues of subsidies, managed trade, procurement and other instruments of industrial policy may have to be joined in FTA discussions, within the context of consultation about the adjustment challenges faced by North American industries and communities, if they are to be most effectively tackled.

The Historical Context

Since the late 1840s when Britain abandoned imperial preferences and the colonial mercantile system, Canadian governments have faced the challenge of framing policies that balance the benefits Canada may receive from further economic integration with the United States and its efforts to build a distinctive, independent North American society.

At times, Ottawa has sought to manage, slow or even reverse the process of bilateral integration through tariffs, industrial policies and preferential trading arrangements with Britain and other Commonwealth countries. Conversely, at other times, Ottawa has taken steps to enhance economic ties with the United States in response to changes in the prospects for Canadian resource exports, the constraints imposed on Canadian industries by technology and market size, and the challenges and opportunities posed by swings in U.S. trade and industrial policies.

Four sets of historical observations, which may be gleaned from Chapters 1 and 2, seem most germane. First, the United States and Canada have approached trade negotiations from fundamentally different perspectives. For example, since the end of World War II, U.S. trade officials have seen bilateral and multilateral negotiations as exercises in economic rationalism, offering opportunities to strengthen the role of markets in shaping patterns of trade and specialization, enhance U.S. market access abroad and impose some external discipline on U.S. import policy.[2]

Extreme economic nationalists notwithstanding, Canadians generally recognize the merits of such thinking. Yet, balancing economic needs against the preservation of national unity and sovereignty pose important challenges for Canadians, as they formulate trade and industrial policies and negotiate with the United States. This will continue to be an enduring theme as the two countries implement and expand the FTA.

Second, although a bold step for Canada and the United States, the FTA is not the first such initiative since the end of the Imperial Trading System in the 1840s. The Reciprocal Trade Agreement of 1854, the Reciprocal Trade Agreements of 1935 and 1938, the Defence Production Sharing Agreement of 1959, and the Automotive Agreement of 1965 also deserve some standing as bench marks in bilateral trade relations.

More importantly, though, none of the aforementioned agreements took place, in the absence of significant changes in the fundamental conditions perceived by Canadians as defining their international trading options. On the Canadian side, each initiative had origins in one or more of the following:

- secular changes in the prospects for Canadian resource exports;

- major changes in the constraints imposed by technology and market size on Canadian industry—e.g., the defence industry in the 1950s and the automobile industry in the 1960s;

- seminal events in British and American commercial policies—e.g., the British retreat from Imperial Preferences in the 1840s and from free trade and the most-favoured-nation principle in the 1920s and 1930s, the U.S. Reciprocal Trade Agreements Act of 1934, and the growing American fascination with contingent protection since the 1970s.

These kinds of developments caused Canadians to review their options with regard to the United States and alter policy.

Meanwhile, for the United States, each of the broad agreements negotiated with Canada since it abandoned a general policy of protectionism in the mid-1930s—the Reciprocal Trade Agreements of 1935 and 1938, the failed agreement of 1948, and the FTA—were generally compatible with its long-term multilateral objectives.

From the late 1960s through the 1980s, shifts in global comparative advantages, technological change, American policies, and the demise of the special relationship significantly altered the constraints and opportunities facing Canadian policy makers. As compared to earlier postwar years, Canadian policy makers adopted a fundamentally modified view of the competitiveness of their resource and manufacturing sectors[3] and the threats posed by recurrent fits of American protectionism. U.S. policy makers saw a trade agreement with Canada as a potential enhancement of their broader multilateral interests.

The successful conclusion of the FTA negotiations owed much to:

- Canadian assessments that resource wealth alone would no longer guarantee prosperity and that the necessary restructuring of Canadian manufacturing was being held hostage to the threat of an American retreat into protectionism.

- U.S. perceptions that American competitiveness problems resulted in no small measure from foreign commercial policies and that a trade agreement with Canada could help progress towards remedial steps in the Uruguay Round.

The third historical observation is that the divergence of Canadian and American trade and industrial policies from the late 1960s to the early 1980s led Americans to interpret Canadian actions by placing considerable emphasis on lesser (greater) Canadian allegiance to market (statist) solutions. Such thinking is wrong-headed. It fails to see the events of the last generation as part of a longer historical continuum in which interventionist policies have ebbed and flowed in both countries, and it fails to consider the potential consequences of yet another welling of nationalist sentiments in the United States.

In both countries, approaches to trade and industrial policy have been and will continue to be the product of the tensions between economic and political imperatives. For Americans, these imperatives have been shaped, over the decades, by the prevailing economic ideology, perceptions of European and Asian industrial capabilities and policies, and American perceptions of their global responsibilities. For Canadians, such considerations also have been important, but their situation is considerably complicated by the scope and weight of American influence on their national life, and ultimately is constrained by American policies.

Fourth, Canada must devote more energy and resources to the bilateral relationship than the United States, because it has more at stake. This is reflected over and over again, for example, in the size of staff assigned by External Affairs and the Department of Finance to the political and economic relationship, and in the resources and national attention devoted to the FTA negotiations. Reflecting on the FTA discussions, Canadian Trade Negotiator Michael Hart has commented that it is commonplace in bilateral negotiations for American politicians to provide the enthusiasm and Canadian officials the vision and details.[4] Often, the United States establishes the environment for bilateral interactions with its multilateral policies, whereas Canadians instigate the key events by adjusting to American actions. Consider, for example, the Reciprocal Trade Agreements Act of 1934—Canada quickly took up the U.S. challenge and negotiated an agreement the following year. The contemporary American drift towards protection caused Canada to seek the FTA.

New Realities

Looking to the future, Canada's basic goal for the FTA—open and secure access to the U.S. market—will endure. For this to be fully realized, the agreement, which is described in Chapter 3, must be fleshed out. Follow-on negotiations on issues such as subsidies, dumping and procurement must yield tangible results—the threat of contingent protection[5] must be dispatched once and for all. As flaws in the agreement become apparent, these will require attention. However, developments in the global economy, by affecting broader U.S. and Canadian competitive prospects and instigating industrial policies, will importantly influence bilateral commercial relations and FTA negotiations.

As discussed in Chapters 4 and 5, growing competitive pressures on North American resource industries and an end to U.S. dominance in many high technology activities are causing both the U.S. and Canadian economies to move towards greater emphasis on mature manufacturing activities, increasing the incidence of bilateral competition among communities for investment and jobs.

In the United States, perceived Japanese intransigence in international negotiations, declining competitiveness in formerly strong export industries and grudging respect for Japanese industrial and technological accomplishments are giving impetus to revisionist critics of U.S. trade policy and advocates of more proactive industrial and innovation policies.

A view is taking hold among a vocal minority within the U.S. trade policy community that market-oriented approaches are inappropriate for managing trade relations with Japan—the Structural Impediments Initiative talks are a manifestation of this view. It is easy to see how such approaches could spill over into trade relations with other countries, making the strength of FTA provisions regarding safeguards and grey-area measures even more critical for Canada.[6] In the context of a legitimate U.S. federal budget deficit reduction program, it is possible that the United States could seek "managed solutions" to trade imbalances with Japan and other East Asian countries, while continuing market-oriented approaches to relations with other trading partners. Such a dichotomy would be difficult to sustain. In any case, Canada's interests would be affected.

Although it is certainly true that U.S. government support has played some considerable role in the emergence of many U.S. capabilities in high-technology industries, the Japanese challenge is fermenting what may yet prove to be a radical change in

American business ideology and U.S. government industrial policy. Key congressional and corporate leaders increasingly advocate Japanese-style innovation policies including greater government assistance for generic precompetitive research and cooperative efforts among business rivals, sometimes with government help and direction, to develop new products and processes. Even among the largest U.S. multinational corporations, alliances to develop, make and market products are becoming ubiquitous.

During the Reagan Administration, Washington quietly experimented with more proactive policies, helping bankroll commercial research in microelectronics, computers, machine tools, advanced manufacturing techniques, and high-definition television, and taking assertive steps to assure greater commercial payoffs from its considerable investments in national laboratories, defence spending and university R & D.

President Bush, influenced by economic advisers John Sununu, Richard Darman and Michael Boskin, has distanced himself from such approaches.[7] However, with some of America's largest industrial corporations and powerful congressmen seeking new initiatives, the pressure for proactive innovation policies will continue. To the extent that they mature into a more aggressive U.S. industrial policy, such policies will have an important impact on Canadian policy options.

For Canada, exclusion from these processes and programs could have the same kind of negative effects on its industrial structure as did foreign tariffs that escalated with the stage of production in earlier postwar decades. Should the United States launch an organized national R & D strategy, requirements for foreign firms to domicile research facilities in the United States to participate in government-assisted ventures could pose considerable problems for Canadian businesses and pose difficult challenges for Canadian policy makers.

Regarding developments in Europe and East Asia, the extension of regional trading arrangements there are providing EC and Japanese industries with larger and diverse markets. Moreover, the combination of EC (Japanese) capital and technology and inexpensive Eastern European (Southeast Asian) labour provides a competitive potential not present within the Canada-U.S. free trade area. In terms of its potential market and rapidly improving, inexpensive labour force, not to mention U.S. geopolitical concerns, Mexico has become an attractive partner for a bilateral trade agreement with the United States. Canada would have a strong stake in such an arrangement.

Turning to the aftermath of the 1990 Meech Lake debate, a more autonomous Quebec could have a variety of effects on the FTA and bilateral relations. However, as indicated in Chapter 6, devolution of economic authority to Quebec or all the provinces should be seen in the light of broader trends, including the increasing assertiveness of the U.S. states regarding industrial policy making.

The Place of the Free Trade Agreement

The FTA does far more than eliminate tariffs and achieve incremental progress on non-tariff barriers. It re-establishes the special relationship between Canada and the United States. What is really significant, though, is that it does so in ways that are responsive to, and compatible with, the policy environment of the 1990s.

As Chapters 1, 2 and 6 point out, private-sector initiatives and the states have come to play increasingly important roles in the formulation of U.S. trade and industrial policies.

During the 1970s and 1980s, successive revisions in U.S. trade remedy laws increased the ease of private access to the U.S. system of contingent protection. Along with the declining importance of tariffs and statutory quotas as a result of GATT tariff negotiations and rules, private suits brought before quasi-judicial bodies in the International Trade Commission and the Commerce Department played an increasingly prominent role in the definition of U.S. import policy. By the late 1970s, Canadian vulnerability to the U.S. system of contingent protection became the primary focus of Canadian concern regarding U.S. trade policy.

Regarding industrial policy, as the Reagan Administration reduced support for various regional and export development programs in the 1980s, the states stepped into the void, developing many of the kinds of programs the provinces had put in place in the 1970s. Moreover, a new activist philosophy has taken hold among the governors, creating new federal-state tensions at the bureaucratic level and intensifying state/provincial competition for industry.

Contingent protection created problems that are not easily managed by the kind of Ottawa-to-Washington interactions which characterized the pre-FTA bilateral relationship. As discussed in Chapter 6, the FTA provides Canada with special status within the U.S. system of contingent protection—the same applies for the United States regarding Canadian trade laws. It establishes a contractual basis for assuring that Canadian (U.S.) firms are not unfairly penalized by U.S. (Canadian) administrative agencies.

Similarly, the two national governments cannot address the problems of state and provincial aids to industry alone—an effective discipline requires the participation of the states and the provinces together. Moreover, not all state/provincial aids are harmful, but drawing lines to craft a subsidies discipline is difficult. FTA follow-on negotiations provide a forum for discussion of these issues.

If Washington takes new initiatives in industrial policy, it will likely be through a more aggressive innovation policy. In the wake of the FTA, the Congress and the U.S. private sector have indicated an initial recognition of a special status for Canada—one of partnership established by the movement towards a single market under the FTA. As discussed in Chapters 5 and 6, Canadian participation in more aggressive U.S. support for R&D through an exchange of national treatment for their multinational corporations (MNCs) may prove an attractive option for Canada.

Similarly, as Washington goes forward with trade negotiations with Mexico, the FTA provides a good point of departure for those talks, now that Canada has joined the talks. From the U.S. perspective, including Canada in the process may make talks more complicated, but the end product would prove more valuable and worth the extra transaction costs. Separate U.S. and Canadian arrangements with Mexico, instead of an evolving joint Mexican-U.S.-Canadian agreement, would likely yield fewer longer term benefits.

Overall, the FTA provides a forum and focal point to address and resolve the issues that will emerge in bilateral relations in a more effective and timely fashion. It can also bring about new arrangements that could reduce the incidence and intensity of problems. Finally, the FTA is a vehicle for opening new avenues of economic cooperation.

Notes

1. With the rise in the exchange rate for the U.S. dollar and U.S. current account deficits, the U.S. share of Canadian exports rose from 69 per cent in 1979 to 79 per cent in 1985; by 1990 it was 75 per cent. Source: *Bank of Canada Review* (April 1990).

2. These efforts have not always proved successful, as politically powerful regional and sectoral groups frequently enjoy strong support in Congress. Exerting pressure on the administration, industries such as textiles and apparel have avoided major tariff reductions and/or have been insulated by managed trade agreements and other forms of contingent protection such as subsidy/countervailing duties and anti-dumping duties.

3. This is most effectively seen by comparing the conclusions of the 1957 Gordon and 1985 Macdonald Royal Commissions with regard to prospects for resource and manufacturing industries.

4. From comments delivered at the Ontario Centre for International Business Conference on Subsidies in America, Toronto, Ontario, November 1, 1989.

5. Contingent protection includes remedies available under U.S. trade laws such as safeguard tariffs and quotas, subsidy/countervailing duties, and antidumping duties. They also include grey-area measures (e.g., orderly marketing agreements and voluntary restraint agreements) that may be precipitated by the threat of actions under trade remedy laws.

6. These grey-area measures include various orderly marketing agreements and voluntary restraint agreements as well as other informal arrangements used to limit trade.

7. Gerald F. Seib and David Wessel, "Three Free Marketeers Shape Bush's Domestic and Economic Policy," *The Wall Street Journal* (April 27, 1990), p. A-1 and A-7.

Chapter 1

Approaches to Commercial Policy

Although the United States and Canada share a continent, some common cultural origins, a language, and many traditions, they have cultivated different public values regarding the individual and the state. Divergent political origins have been important. Americans draw their intellectual substance from the Eighteenth Century liberal underpinnings of the American Revolution, while English Canadians, with their significant Loyalist heritage, have adopted more British traditions, practices and concepts of ordered society. The Quebecois for their part have sought to preserve a French nation in North America. In important ways, the national cultures that emerged in English and French Canada are reactions to, albeit rejections of, the American Revolution and The Conquest.

According to Seymour Martin Lipset:

Canada has been a more conservative, traditional, law abiding, statist, and elitist society than the United States.[1]

Geography has played an important role in Canada's development. Canada has had to address some different challenges to the United States. Its extensive land mass, more difficult environment, later western settlement, and smaller population neces-

13

sitated more recent and sustained government involvement in the provision of services "for which sufficient private capital or a profitable market has not been available."[2] Importantly, in the context of bilateral commercial relations, Canadian governments have taken steps to insulate Canadian industries from American competition to ensure the survival and vitality of essential national economic and cultural institutions.

In the Canadian experience, the mandates of economic rationalism generally have been well recognized but counterbalanced in policy by the requirements of building and maintaining a separate nation. This said, in looking to the future, it is easy to make too much of such distinctions between Canada and the United States. In particular, simplistic conclusions about the consequences of the Canadian nation-building imperative and the resulting future tensions between Canadian and U.S. policies are fraught with dangers.

For example, although the United States has generally shown more affinity for market solutions than Canada since the end of World War II, to characterize Canadians as merely more interventionist or statist than Americans is to gloss over important subtleties about why policies are made, to ignore the lessons of the longer sweep of history, and in the process, to miss important clues about where the two societies may be headed.

Over the last two centuries, both nations have faced the tasks of settling a wilderness, developing abundant resources, assimilating immigrants from many cultures, and becoming more integrated into the international economy as their industrial maturity and broader national interests warranted. For both federal governments, economic policy entailed a strong component of nation building. The latter imperative has not been unique to Canada, just more recent, and hence, in our own times, more compelling.

Looking to the future, as the global and economic pressures acting on the two countries change and domestic perceptions of resulting challenges emerge, national approaches to policy ultimately will follow assessments of national interests—governing ideologies frame and colour policies but ultimately change, for better or worse, becoming more or less nationalistic/interventionist/protectionist/predatory when prevailing policies fail to deliver desired outcomes.

In this context, one can say much about what has been distinctive about the two countries' approaches to trade and industrial policy since the end of World War II. What is important to consider, though, is how the challenges facing policy makers continue to change and the consequences they may have for future policies and bilateral interactions.

U.S. Trade Policy in the Postwar Era

Tensions in U.S. Policy and the Free Trade Agreement

In the postwar era, bilateral trade and investment have fostered patterns of production and specialization that exploit regional comparative advantages. Through much of this century, the United States has imported from Canada substantial amounts of asbestos, nickel, wood pulp, and newsprint. During and after World War II, increased imports from and direct investment in Canada permitted the United States to substitute Canadian copper, lead and zinc for depleting U.S. deposits and to limit its strategic vulnerability. As an expression of their affinity for market solutions, U.S. officials have encouraged their Canadian counterparts to take actions that facilitate the freer flow of goods and capital. In interpreting and responding to Canadian policies, often American officials have been puzzled, critical or even hostile when Canadians have chosen more *dirigiste* approaches.

The U.S. has been the principle architect of the postwar international economic and political systems. In this role the persistent preoccupations of U.S. negotiators in the GATT and elsewhere have been the liberalization of markets for goods and capital and the systemic codification of market disciplines. These goals importantly influence U.S. approaches to bilateral relations and U.S. reactions to Canadian actions, especially when the latter have been perceived as dissonant with broader American goals. Consider, for example, U.S. concerns during the early 1980s that key aspects of Canada's foreign investment and energy policies could set precedents for other U.S. relationships, or that special considerations under U.S. trade law sought by Canada in the free trade negotiations could trigger problems for the United States with other GATT signatories.

In light of the recent history of bilateral commercial relations (including hot disputes over Canada's Foreign Investment Review Agency, the National Energy Program, regional and industrial subsidies, and cultural policies) and the Mulroney government's subsequent rejection of most aspects of economic nationalism, the Canada-U.S. Free Trade Agreement (FTA) could be simplistically characterized as a Canadian accession to the U.S. market paradigm. The latter is perhaps conditioned on U.S. acknowledgment of special Canadian needs with regard to cultural industries, investment and more stability, and a greater role in interpreting, the rules of the game. However, such a generalization entails a naive characterization of American policy—paradigm and policy are seldom identical—and interpretation of Canadian responses.

The cleavage in the American system between the global and national interests of the administration, and regional and sectoral concerns of the Congress have made U.S. trade policy less than true to *laissez faire* principles. It has become a peculiar mixture of a general championing of liberalization and market disciplines in the GATT and elsewhere and protectionist concessions to special interests at home.

Just as in Canada, in the United States commercial policy reflects a balancing of competing goals and interests. It reflects the aspirations of successive Republican and Democratic administrations and their internationalist allies in the Congress to build a liberal international economic system on the one hand, and the concerns of congressmen and senators with constituents in import-injured and declining industries on the other. The FTA reflects this tension—consider the endurance of informal export controls on Canadian steel and the export tax on Canadian softwood lumber.

Fundamentally, the FTA is a political commitment by both national governments to articulate jointly and enforce the rules of bilateral commerce. The overarching goal and thrust of these rules is to be liberalization consistent with and an extension of GATT principles. Yet the FTA's provisions, mirroring the trade policies of both nations, embody concessions to domestic political sensitivities concerning industrial and regional adjustment as well as concessions to Canada's concerns about economic and cultural sovereignty. In particular, consider the provisions regarding investment screening and the exclusion of cultural industries from most FTA disciplines.

Concessions to domestic sensitivities are not surprising. Jointly articulated rules, in addition to removing barriers, seek to define limits on the degree to which economic interest in either country may fall victim to political pressures for new protection in the other. The corollary effect is that joint rules for bilateral commerce, like domestic policies, must strike a balance between broad national goals and the regionally-, industrially- and geographically-motivated political imperatives acting on the two federal executives. The United States and Canada will proceed with follow-on negotiations to flesh out the provisions of the FTA. Their efforts to frame joint rules for subsidies, procurement and other instruments of industrial policy will have to reflect both the logic of liberalization and systemic disciplines on the one hand, and domestic pressures on Washington and Ottawa to assuage the adjustment burdens imposed by global competition and accelerating technological change on the other hand.

The Origins and Outlook for U.S. Policy

In retrospect, the U.S. slide towards protectionism in the 1970s and 1980s is not surprising. Prior to the 1930s, the United States could be characterized as at least as protectionist as Canada—U.S. tariffs on dutiable imports were generally much higher than Canadian duties.[3] During the period of Britain's industrial dominance in the Nineteenth Century, the U.S. government vigorously protected American industry.

This policy of protectionism did not have the same adverse consequences for the U.S. industrial structure as the National Policy did for Canada because of the continental size of the U.S. market and the fairly limited number of other Nineteenth Century nations with advanced industrial capabilities. The Nineteenth Century American market provided adequate scope for economies of scale and the discipline of competition, at least prior to formation of the great trusts.

With the Reciprocal Trade Agreements Act of 1934, the United States replaced Britain as principal champion of trade liberalization and the most-favoured-nation principle.[4] During the early postwar era, U.S. support for a liberal trading order had its origins in the overarching U.S. foreign policy objective of establishing a system of interdependent nation states in the West, as a requisite for building a permanent peace and as a counter-weight to Soviet expansionism.[5] A program of multilateral tariff reductions was strongly supported by the U.S. trade policy community, namely the amalgamation of international lawyers, academics, journalists, and civil servants who enjoy considerable influence in Washington. The lessons of the Depression and modern (neoclassical) international economics forged a consensus within this group that in the long run freer trade fosters the most desirable patterns of international specialization, economic development and growth.

Until the Kennedy Round, opposition to trade liberalization from industry groups was dampened by the large trade surpluses, American postwar industrial dominance and the peril-point provision of U.S. trade legislation, which prohibited tariff cuts below levels determined by the Tariff Commission as necessary for the viability of domestic industries.

In 1955 Jacob Viner commented that duty reductions under the Reciprocal Trade Agreements Program had been little more than window dressing. While this was an exaggeration (consider, for example, average tariffs on dutiable imports fell from 53 per cent in 1934 to 12 per cent in 1952), it does indicate the kind of turning point that Kennedy Round *linear* tariff cuts were for U.S. tariff policy and the GATT.[6]

The Trade Expansion Act of 1962 dropped the peril-point, no-injury approach, and promised adjustment assistance for workers displaced by imports. The Kennedy Round (1964-67) resulted in a 35 per cent lowering of U.S. tariffs in stages from 1968 to 1972. In the 1970s, these cuts, along with the emergence of Japan and the newly industrializing countries as major exporters in many mature and highly unionized industries—e.g., textiles, apparel, steel, footwear, consumer electronics, and automobiles—and the ineffectiveness of trade adjustment assistance, were among the principal factors causing the labour movement and communities dependent on these industries to lobby aggressively for protection.

During the 1970s and 1980s, U.S. trade remedy laws had been refined by Congress, increasing opportunities for distressed industries and workers to receive import relief under the safeguard (escape) clause,[7] dumping, countervailing duty, and unfair trade practices provisions of U.S. trade laws. Increasingly, private actions have driven U.S. trade policy.

By the late 1980s, the U.S. textile, apparel, automobile, and steel industries were the beneficiaries of managed trade agreements. U.S. trade measures or threatened trade measures posed major dangers to Canadian export interests in forest and fish products, basic steel, specialty steel, nonferrous metals, and secondary manufacturing. The vulnerability was apparent of Canadian industrial development goals and policies to the U.S. system of contingent protection, most notably U.S. trade measures initiated by private actions.

Successive administrations have remained committed to the GATT system and have resisted the tightening of trade laws and special import restrictions. Yet political pressures, such as those brought by the Congress and in key states during presidential elections, have caused successive presidents to yield in the industries noted above.

Consider, for example, the campaign statements of candidates Kennedy, Reagan and Bush about textiles, automobiles and steel during their 1960, 1980 and 1988 campaigns, as well as President Reagan's decision to roll back "unfair trade" in steel with voluntary restraint agreements in October 1984. Recent administrations have lobbied strenuously against tightening trade laws, however, they are constrained in their discretion in applying these laws once passed.

Presidents have the greatest latitude with regard to Section 201 of the 1974 Trade Act[8] and in the framing of voluntary restraint agreements to avoid actions under 201 or other provisions of U.S. law. In this context, presidents have generally been able to resist permanent non-tariff protection for industries other than those noted above, which are large and geographically dispersed, and hence widely represented in the senate and electoral college. Consider, for example, the frustrations of the footwear, furniture and nonferrous metals industries in this regard.[9]

In recent years, the consensus for trade liberalization within the U.S. trade policy community has been further weakened by some scepticism about:

- the ability of the GATT to address non-tariff issues of major concern to the United States;

- Japanese and European[10] resolve to pursue multilateral trade liberalization;

- the efficacy of the free trade paradigm itself.

As for Japan, revisionists views are taking hold that:

> Japan is really different—and that conventional free trade policies won't work. Once these views would have been dismissed as "Japan-bashing," but now they have an intellectual base.[11]

Focusing on the free trade paradigm, the new theory of "strategic trade policy" put forward by several leading economists resurrects the classical infant industry justification for protection, adapting it to high-technology industries.[12] Although international economists are generally skeptical about governments' ability to effectively apply their prescriptions, it provides cannon fodder for proponents of more interventionist American policies. Within the business community, traditional aversions to government-business cooperation and industry consortia have eroded, and the Reagan Administration sought to refocus its considerable spending for defence, space exploration and basic research into a commercial R & D war chest.[13] Acceptance of Japanese models, along with revisionist views of Japan and international trade theory, erode support for liberal trade policies.

Similarly, hardening attitudes and Japanese vocalization that U.S. trade and industrial problems are most fundamentally related to U.S. fiscal policies, poor U.S. saving performance, cultural shortcomings among American managers and workers, and the declining performance of American primary and secondary schools adds to pressures in the Congress to abandon liberal trade policies.

In this context, U.S. objectives with regard to Canada remain clear. The administration has an earnest desire to lower bilateral trade barriers and to use the FTA, with Canada, to define jointly and enforce rules in what is now an exceedingly complex commercial relationship. However, protectionist pressures in the United States may be cresting, implying immediate but not enduring danger to Canadian interests. More likely, though, these pressures are swelling, potentially constraining Washington's ability to deal reasonably with Ottawa and implying a far more complex policy challenge for Canada.

Should the Uruguay Round and bilateral talks with Japan fail to deliver substantial improvements in market access abroad, the likelihood rises that the United States will continue its slide towards more interventionist trade and/or industrial policies. A more aggressive American industrial policy, focused on the creation and application of new technologies, could insulate the president, somewhat, from sectarian interests in the Congress. The president could find pressures for import measures in mature industries easier to deflect if he is advocating or at least accepting more widely supportable Japanese-style approaches to promoting high-technology activities. If the administration truly wants to curb the use of Section 201 measures and voluntary restraint agreements, the flow of ideas and events could make direct assistance to industries—e.g., to high-technology business consortia through procurement and subsidies—a politically pragmatic and attractive approach.

In contrast to the Reagan Administration, the Bush Administration has resisted pressure to adopt more aggressive innovation policies, (see Chapter 4) but a number of federal and state programs are underway and warrant careful monitoring by Canada.

Such actions, taken in response to Japanese and European Community competition, would not be as likely to sideswipe directly Canadian firms and workers as U.S. import measures in mature industries. Rather, the danger to Canada could lie in the exclusion of Canadian companies. Canadian high-technology firms would be at an enormous disadvantage if they were frozen out of U.S. consortia or denied access to U.S. procurement, aggressively focused to promote the competitiveness of selected industries such as high-definition TV. Unlike safeguard, dumping and countervailing duty actions, the challenge for Canadian policy makers would not be how to insulate Canadian interests from U.S. protection but how to achieve the inclusion of Canadian enterprises in the benefits flowing from an American industrial policy. In this context, a more aggressive U.S. policy would alter Canadian objectives in FTA negotiations on issues such as subsidies and procurement.

In another vein, a continued U.S. interest in other bilateral initiatives parallel these trends. In particular, the U.S. economic and political stake in Mexican economic reforms requires the United States to respond favourably to Mexico's desire to negotiate a bilateral agreement. Regardless of whether the Uruguay Round achieves significant progress and whether the United States continues to lead the drive for multilateral liberalization or adopts a sceptical approach to the GATT in the 1990s, U.S. efforts to frame arrangements to increase trade and investment with Mexico seem inevitable. U.S. policy will continue to run on two tracks—multilateral and bilateral.

Canadian Approaches to Policy

Through most of the Twentieth Century, bilateral trade and investment ties have grown steadily, and Canadian industries have become increasingly dependent on U.S. markets and capital. Although the United States sold Canada three-fifths of its imports in 1900, the United States accounted for only about one-third of Canada's exports. The U.S. share of Canadian exports increased to more than two-thirds in 1958 and about three-fourths in 1989.[14]

The role and influence of U.S. multinational corporations (MNCs) moved on a parallel track. In 1900, the American and British shares of non-resident Canadian investment were 14 and 85 per cent, respectively. In the 1920s, Americans moved into first position, increasing their share to more than half. This increased to well over 75 per cent after World War II.[15]

Balancing Canadian Objectives

The dominance of U.S. products, the pervasive presence of U.S. MNCs in Canadian mining and manufacturing, U.S. cultural and political influences, and lingering (though diminishing) affinity among English Canadians for British connections have given rise to varying amounts of ambivalence among Canadians about the growth of bilateral commerce. What some observers see as a trend towards efficiency-building, wealth-creating interdependence, others see as a dangerous tilt towards dependency. Generally, Canadian policy makers have sought to balance the economic benefits of further integration with the affluent U.S. market and concerns about maintaining the vitality and integrity of distinctive Canadian economic, cultural and political institutions.

At various times in this century, the Canadian government has taken steps to limit the pace of integration with the U.S. markets. High Canadian tariffs through the Tokyo Round were one obvious tool. Prior to World War II, other policies included Canada's persistent efforts to re-establish a British preferential trading system. For example, Canada unilaterally extended preferences to members of the British Empire in 1897.[16] It continued to press for reciprocal access to the British market through the 1930s, despite Britain's free trade posture. It negotiated preferential arrangements with other dominions and played a leading role at the Ottawa Conference of 1932, which essentially established a new British preferential system.[17] In 1907, Canada established a three-tier tariff with U.S. products being charged the highest rates.[18] In fact, for the brief period between the Ottawa Conference and the Canadian-American Trade Agreement of 1935, there is some evidence that these policies contributed to a diversion of Canadian trade towards Great Britain at the expense of the United States.[19]

More recently, Canadian industrial, foreign investment and energy policies, which emerged in the late 1960s and reached their zenith in the early 1980s, had among their principal goals the reduction of Canada's economic dependence on the United States— the so-called "Third Option."

Historically, this exercise in political economy has been strongly influenced by Canadian assessments of:

- the strength of international markets for Canadian resource products—the rents from these resource exports helped offset the costs of protecting other industries;

- the constraints imposed by market size and technology on import-competing manufacturing;

- major changes in the trade policies of Canada's principal partners, the United States and Great Britain.

The Ottawa Conference and its Aftermath

In the years following the U.S. Smoot-Hawley tariff (1930), Canada's Dunning and Bennett tariffs (1930) and Britain's Abnormal Importations Act (1931) and Import Duties Act (1932),[20] the United States and Britain changed places in terms of trade emphasis. During the prosperity of the 1920s, the United States "was undergoing one of those periods of high protection, which have always had severe repercussions for Canada."[21] Although Britain's free trade posture eroded somewhat with the Safeguard Key Industries Act of 1921, it did not abandon a truly liberal policy posture until the early 1930s. Subsequently, as major trading nations sought to renegotiate tariffs, Britain and the United States took different tacks. At the 1932 Ottawa Commonwealth Conference, Britain concurred to re-establish, and subsequently sought to maintain, a preferential trading system with its former colonies.

Shortly thereafter, U.S. Secretary of State Cordell Hull made the most-favoured-nation principle the basis of the new U.S. trade liberalization program initiated with the Reciprocal Trade Agreements Act of 1934. As Dana Wilgress observed:

> By making the [most-favoured-nation] clause the basis of his policy, Mr. Cordell Hull signified that the United States had taken over from Great Britain the task of being the main proponent of this principle.[22]

After gaining preferential access to the British market, Canada sought negotiations with the United States under the new law. In them, it worked for exemptions for its British preferences. In the Canadian-American trade agreements of 1935 and 1938, as well as the British-American agreement of 1938, the United States accepted British preferences as exceptions to the most-favoured-nation principle, although some margins of preference were reduced. By readjusting its policy objectives, in response to altered policies in the United States and Britain, Canada was able to balance its relationships with its two major partners. It improved its access to the U.S. market while continuing to favour trade with Britain.

Although the exemption of British preferences to the most-favoured-nation principle was later grandfathered in the GATT, these preferences declined in importance with successive rounds of GATT-sponsored tariff reductions. Canada turned to the GATT and other postwar institutions to find counterweights to its dependence on U.S. markets and capital.

Postwar Adjustments

The years immediately following World War II witnessed a reduction in Canada's sales to the devastated British economy. Eventually, increased U.S. purchases of Canadian metals and minerals would replace reduced exports to Britain. However, during the adjustment period (1946-47), Canada experienced considerable balance of payments difficulties (a dollar shortage) and was forced to restrict some imports and seek official financial assistance from the United States in the form of a loan from the Export-Import Bank. The United States also permitted $1 billion of Marshall Plan funds to be spent in Canada.

Apparently perceiving a temporary current account problem to be permanent, strong interest emerged among Canadian policy makers in establishing closer economic ties with the United States. John Deutsch, Canada's chief negotiator in secret bilateral talks, wrote to a colleague:

> The intention in Ottawa is to try to work out further tariff cuts, particularly in the manufactured goods field, which would make possible a better balance in the enormous one-way trade associated with our branch plants.[23]

Canada's negotiators were apparently concerned about its industry becoming permanently dependent on import restrictions.[24]

By early 1948, a free trade or arrangement area emerged as the likely outcome. However, as Canada's balance of payments problems subsided (thanks in part to Marshall Plan sales), Mackenzie King developed second thoughts about the political consequences of establishing closer ties with the United States. On March 24, while considering a free trade agreement proposed by negotiators, he wrote in his diary:

> . . . while it might be sound economically, I believed it would be fatal politically.[25]

The negotiations were terminated.

Through the 1950s, massive growth in U.S. investments in and imports from Canada's mining and smelting industries provided new sources of American dollars and eliminated the need for a new trade arrangement with the United States or for reorienting Canada's domestically-focused manufacturing industries (the branch plants referred to by Deutsch) towards the U.S. market. Free trade would re-emerge when Canadians once again perceived their export opportunities as fundamentally altered and constrained, and saw secure, free access to the U.S. market as a necessity.

Canada and the United States turned their attention to the newly formed GATT where they became partners in advocating a global system of rules for trade. For middle powers like Canada, the GATT offers opportunities to form alliances with countries sharing common interests, thereby achieving some leverage in negotiations with larger powers such as the United States and the EC. Also, the GATT offers opportunities to open non-U.S. markets to diversify Canadian exports, and the advantages of multilateral rules, mediation and dispute settlement when issues arise with the United States.

Taking Stock: The Gordon Report

In the late 1950s, after more than a decade of impressive growth in Canadian resource exports to the United States and in American investments in the mining and smelting industries, Canada's policy community attached little urgency to trade liberalization.

According to the landmark 1957 Royal Commission Report on Canada's Economic Prospects (the Gordon Report),[26] Canadians were well aware of the costs imposed by its tariff, but these were more than offset by other, noneconomic benefits:

> One effect of the tariff has clearly been to increase the price to Canadians of many commodities on which duties are levied. More broadly, it must be recognized that in the absence of the tariff there would have been a different and more productive allocation of the factors of production in Canada with a consequent increase in real income per capita . . . .

But, on the whole, Canadians have been willing to pay
the price that the tariff exacts in lower average incomes,
regarding it as a legitimate cost of nationhood.[27]

Moreover, the Commission concluded that these costs were being
reduced, over time, by economic progress.[28]

The whole tone of the Commission's report reflected an
exuberance and confidence that the Canadian economy had
achieved enormous strides in expanding its manufacturing base
since the 1939 Report of the Rowell-Sirois Royal Commission,[29]
and that the prospects for its resource exports remained strong:

> A quite startling rapid growth is in prospect for output
> for the resource industries. This is due to continued
> favourable market opportunities abroad, particularly in
> the United States, and to the large increments which
> have taken place in our knowledge of available
> resources . . . .[30]

These considerations, coupled with considerable Canadian
pessimism about the U.S. inclinations to continue its leadership
role in trade liberalization[31] or to be receptive to a Canadian
overture for bilateral trade talks,[32] caused the Gordon Commission to conclude:

> . . . it would seem sensible for this country to hold the
> tariff line on the average at about its present level.[33]

And the idea of a broad free trade agreement with the United
States was dismissed as impractical:

> . . . broad reciprocity with the United States, in the
> opinion of the Commission, cannot now or in the fore-
> seeable future be regarded as a practical proposition.[34]

The door was left open, however, to other more limited
arrangements.[35] Over the next decade, when it became apparent
that the Canadian market was too small to support a critical
industry without imposing unbearable costs, the Canadian
government sought to negotiate sectoral arrangements with the
United States in defence systems and automobiles.[36]

The Conduct of U.S. Trade Policy and the Special Relationship

In considering the disinclination towards a trade agreement with the United States, it is important to recognize that, in some ways, U.S. trade policy in the 1950s worked very differently from the 1970s and 1980s. The overall environment for Canadian-American relations was also quite different.

In the 1950s, the tariff was the principal means for protecting industries in both countries, and for Canada, the threat of U.S. contingent protection was not yet significant. Specifically, reviewing U.S. trade policies in the 1950s, Brecher and Reisman note the importance of tariffs and the following non-tariff barriers—customs procedures, Buy American practices and the safeguard actions.[37] With the exception of safeguards, these are all practices whose protective effects are not raised or imposed through private suits brought before quasi-judicial government agencies. Safeguard actions were not used to any great effect on Canada in the 1950s.[38]

Tariffs in both countries are subject to GATT tariff bindings. To the extent these could be lowered, Canada could achieve its objectives vis-a-vis the United States in multilateral trade negotiations. In these, government-to-government interactions take precedence over private initiatives, although the private sectors are consulted and do lobby. Generally, tariffs cannot be raised above GATT bindings through private initiatives.

Regarding the non-tariff barriers noted above, the private sector can lobby for import restricting statutory or regulatory changes. Other than in the case of safeguards, the private sector cannot obtain an increase in protection by bringing suit before the Department of Commerce and/or the International Trade Commission. The opposite is true for the U.S. system of contingent protection under U.S. trade remedy laws.

In the 1970s and 1980s, the situation changed fundamentally. Tariffs became much less important. The Tokyo Round limited the use of certain non-tariff devices including customs procedures and procurement. And although the private sector still had some latitude to lobby for more protectionist statutes and regulations, it increasingly sought relief from rising imports through trade remedy laws.

As noted earlier, the number and range of U.S. industries that obtained protection in this fashion became quite impressive. U.S. trade policy had become increasingly driven by private actions, and by the late 1970s, contingent protection emerged as the primary focus of Canadian concern regarding U.S. policy.

Dealing with contingent protection did not lend itself effectively to government-to-government management or to quick redress through GATT-sponsored multilateral negotiations. Canada could only address it in a timely fashion through bilateral negotiations—lassoing U.S. contingent protection became one of the central goals for Canadian negotiators in shaping the FTA.

On another level, during the 1950s the special relationship endured, lubricating government-to-government relations. Established in war-time cooperation, Canada and the United States consulted closely on foreign policy, and so Canada could expect some special consideration from the United States when the larger partner took broader policy actions. For example, after World War II, when Canada encountered balance of payments difficulties with the decline of exports to Great Britain, the United States permitted, as noted, some Marshall Plan funds to be spent in Canada.

By the 1970s, the United States had determined it could no longer afford or was no longer inclined to afford Canada such special treatment. This also affected the impact of government-to-government contacts in resolving and pre-empting disputes.

Economic Nationalism and the Rationale for Policy

During the 1950s, the tariff continued to give Canadian manufacturing substantial protection and was the principal instrument of industrial policy. Canada had little in the way of industrial development programs intended to move resources into particular activities or steer economic growth along politically-desired paths. It generally welcomed and did little to regulate U.S. investment and the growth of its resource exports to the United States. The primary role of government policy was to maintain a favourable macroeconomic environment for growth and price stability.[39] Unlike the period of the National Policy of the 1920s, the federal government offered few bounties or subsidies to industry.[40]

In the 1960s, concerns emerged about Canada's heavy reliance on resource exports, the need to further strengthen manufacturing, and regional imbalances in income and employment opportunities. These issues coincided with growing concerns about the potentially adverse consequences of U.S. ownership in mining and manufacturing on exports, R & D performance and employment opportunities, as well as the pervasive presence of the U.S. media and other American cultural influences on Canada's national life. It must be remembered, in the space of just one generation, foreign control of Canadian mining and manufacturing had jumped from about 40 per cent in 1938 to more than 60 per cent in 1963,[41] and the television had emerged as a major force in North American life, with U.S. programs dominating the airwaves.

Strains in the special relationship emerged. Canadian and American views on foreign policy and the cold war diverged more often, especially with regard to Vietnam. Prime Minister Diefenbaker, concerned about the growth of American influence in Canada, had a strained relationship with President Kennedy. After his Temple University speech criticizing U.S. bombing of North Vietnam on April 2, 1965, Prime Minister Pearson's relationship with President Johnson became what one journalist called a "Burlesque Circus."[42] Ultimately, under Prime Minister Trudeau, a more independent Canadian policy emerged from a major foreign policy assessment. And as U.S. trade problems mounted in the 1970s, apparently the Nixon administration determined that special treatment for Canada was no longer warranted, or that it was something the United States could no longer afford.

Proposals for more interventionist policies emerged. The tariff, and trade policy generally, became part of a broader debate about how Canada could maximize the benefits it received from the bilateral relationship through industrial and investment policies. This national dialogue could be characterized as a tug-of-war between Canadian internationalists, who emphasized the efficiency gains from greater reliance on markets and integration with the U.S. economy, and Canadian nationalists, who often doubted the economic benefits of closer bilateral ties and worried more about the consequences of increased economic ties for Canadian political, economic and cultural sovereignty.[43]

When nationalist views reached their peak in the late 1970s and early 1980s, their prominence called into question a key operating premise of earlier postwar Canadian policy. The Gordon Report articulated a recognition of the economic costs of limiting integration with the U.S. economy. These were the opportunity costs paid by Canadians for the nation-building benefits of the tariff and other national policies. In contrast, some nationalists rejected this basic calculus. In their view, the regulation of trade and investment could quantitatively and qualitatively enhance economic performance—proactive industrial policies could improve the allocation of resources and accelerate growth. This view is distinctly reminiscent of western European concepts of market-responsive, *dirigiste* industrial policies and a precursor of contemporary U.S. sentiments for a more activist innovation policy.

It was not until public acceptance of the nationalist prescriptions declined in the mid-1980s and the economic costs of restraining bilateral trade and investment flows were again broadly accepted, that a bilateral trade agreement became a serious possibility. The question again emerged in mid-1980s for Canadians in terms of what would be the costs of not having a trade agreement and how much an agreement might compromise Canada's distinctive national cultural, social and political institutions.

Notes

1. Seymour Martin Lipset, "Canada and the United States: The Cultural Dimension," in Charles F. Doran and John H. Sigler (eds.), *Canada and the United States: Enduring Friendship, Persistent Stress* (Englewood Cliffs, N.J.: Prentice Hall, Inc., 1985), p. 110.

2. *Ibid.*, pp. 110-111.

3. See the Economic Council of Canada, *Looking Outward: A New Trade Strategy for Canada* (Ottawa: Information Canada, 1975), Chart 1-1, p. 4.

4. The United States began adhering to the unconditional most-favoured-nation principle in trade agreements in 1922. Orville John McDiarmid, *Commercial Policy in the Canadian Economy* (Cambridge, Mass.: Harvard University Press, 1946), p. 289.

5. See for example, Theodore Geiger, *The Future of the International System: The United States and the World Political Economy* (Winchester, Mass: Allen & Unwin, 1988), Chapter 2.

6. For Viner's comments, see *Hearings Before the Subcommittee on Foreign Economic Policy* (Washington, D.C.: U.S. Government Printing Office, 1955) p. 597.

7. Article XIX of the GATT permits signatories to temporarily increase protection to industries that suffer from, or are threatened by, serious injury as a result of an import surge. Section 201 of the Trade Act of 1974 establishes the procedures for U.S. industries to petition the International Trade Commission for temporary increases in tariffs or quotas. It also establishes the standards for proving the presence or threat of serious injury.

8. See footnote 7.

9. With regard to nonferrous metals, in 1984 both the steel and copper industries timed their import relief efforts to coincide with the 1984 presidential campaign. However, only steel, which enjoys much wider representation, succeeded in its objectives.

10. With regard to Europe, concern has emerged that the EC 1992 program, along with expansion of the EC to include Greece, Spain and Portugal, are creating administrative and political distractions and economic adjustments that effectively sap the EC's capacity to pursue trade liberalization. Moreover, EC 1992 provides opportunities, for example, through the standards setting processes and other aspects of regulatory harmonization, to further cement within the EC policy framework continental European *dirigiste* perspectives.

11. See, for example, "Rethinking Japan," *Business Week* (August 7, 1989), pp. 44-52—quote taken from cover.

12. See Peter Morici, *Reassessing American Competitiveness* (Washington, D.C.: National Planning Association, 1988), pp. 44-47, and David J. Richardson, "Strategic Trade Policy: Research and Practice in the United States," in Richard G. Lipsey and Wendy Dobson (eds.), *Shaping Comparative Advantage* (Toronto: C.D. Howe Institute, 1987).

13. See Chapter 4.

14. The U.S. share of Canadian imports rose from 59 per cent in 1900 to 66, 69 and 75 per cent in 1926, 1958 and 1989. The U.S. share of Canadian exports rose from 34 per cent in 1900 to 36, 59 and 70 per cent in 1926, 1958 and 1989. See Grant L. Reuber, *The Growth and Changing Composition of Trade Between the United States and Canada* (Montreal: Canadian American Committee, 1960), p. 14; *Bank of Canada Review* (April 1990).

15. Reuber, *The Growth and Changing Composition of Trade*, p. 14.

16. McDiarmid, in *Commercial Policy in the Canadian Economy*, characterized this initiative as "the most spectacular change in the tariff policy of Canada between 1879 and 1907" (p. 209).

17. See Frank Stone, *Canada, the GATT and the International Trading System* (Montreal: The Institute for Research on Public Policy, 1984), pp. 8-9; and McDiarmid, *Commercial Policy in the Canadian Economy*, Chapters 9 and 11.

18. McDiarmid, *Commercial Policy in the Canadian Economy*, p. 221.

19. In the early 1930s, with the United States, Canada and Britain all imposing high tariffs, the volume of trade declined in all directions. Beginning in 1932, though, tariff preferences were two-way between Canada and Britain. From 1931 to 1934, the U.S. share of Canadian exports fell from 43 to 34 per cent, while the British share rose from 28 to 40 per cent. Turning to Canadian imports, the U.S. share fell from 63 to 57 per cent, while the British share rose from 17 to 22 per cent. *Ibid.*, pp. 331-337.

20. The latter two laws reduced the free list from 83 per cent of British imports to about 30 per cent and initiated some preferences to British countries, anticipating the outcome of the Ottawa Conference. See McDiarmid, *Commercial Policy in the Canadian Economy*, pp. 278-279.

21. The principal instruments were the Emergency Tariff (1921) and the Fordney-McCumber Tariff (1922). See L.D. Wilgress, *Canada's Approach to Trade Negotiations* (Montreal: Private Planning Association of Canada, 1963), p. 7.

22. *Ibid.*, p. 8.

23. J.L. Granatstein, "The Course of Canadian-American Relations Since 1945," in Doran and Sigler (eds.), *Canada and the United States*, p. 48.

24. See R.D. Cuff and J.L. Granatstein, *American Dollars—Canadian Prosperity*, (Toronto: Samuel Stevens, 1978), pp. 72-73.

25. *Ibid.*, p. 78.

26. Canada Royal Commission on Canada's Economic Prospects [Gordon Commission], *Final Report November 1957*, (Ottawa: Queen's Printer, 1958).

27. *Ibid.*, pp. 49 and 50.

28. *Ibid.*, p. 445.

29. *Ibid.*, pp. 94-95.

30. *Ibid.*, p. 361.

31. At the time the commissioners were issuing their final report (1957), most of the president's tariff-cutting authority on the Reciprocal Trade Agreements Act had been exhausted in the first four GATT rounds. It was not until the Trade Expansion Act of 1962 that the president had broad latitude to reduce tariffs further.

32. Gordon Commission, *Final Report*, p. 444.

33. *Ibid.*, p. 441.

34. *Ibid.*, p. 445.

35. *Ibid.*

36. In 1959, when it became obvious with the cancellation of the Avro Arrow project that the costs of developing high-technology weapons had escalated beyond the means of a middle-sized industrial country lacking an assured market in North Atlantic Treaty Organization (NATO), Canada entered into the Defence Production Sharing Agreement with the United States. Similarly, by 1965, when the potential for economies of scale made the production of automobiles in Canada for the domestic market increasingly unattractive, even with the benefit of a 17.5 per cent tariff, Canada entered into the Automotive Agreement. These agreements further integrated Canadian and American production, ensuring a continued Canadian presence in these industries.

37. Irving Brecher and Simon S. Reisman, *Canada-U.S. Economic Relations* (Ottawa: Royal Commission on Canada's Economic Prospects, 1957), pp. 170-177.

38. *Ibid.*, p. 177.

39. The final report of the Gordon Commission stated: "As we have said before, we believe that preventing unemployment and avoiding inflation will be the major problem for our government in the field of domestic policy in the future." See *Final Report*, p. 434.

40. See McDiarmid, *Canadian Commercial Policy*, pp. 192-193, 203, 262, and 345.

41. See Brecher and Reisman, *Canada-United States Economic Relations*, p. 101; and A.E. Safarian, *The Performance of Foreign-Owned Firms in Canada* (Montreal: Canadian-American Committee, 1969), p. xviii.

42. Lawrence Martin, *The Presidents and the Prime Ministers* (Toronto: Doubleday Canada Ltd., 1982), Chapter 13.

43. A concise summary of the prevailing arguments for and against free trade may be found in External Affairs, *A Review of Canadian Trade Policy* (Ottawa: Ministry of Supply and Services, 1983), pp. 209-211.

Chapter 2

The Road to Free Trade

Prior to World War II, Canadian trade deficits with the United States were offset, in large measure, by trade surpluses with Great Britain. In 1939, the United States accounted for 66 per cent of Canada's imports but only 41 per cent of its exports, while Britain sold Canada only 15 per cent of its imports yet absorbed 36 per cent of its exports.[1] After the war, Canada's exports to Britain were held up for a while by Marshall Plan sales, but in 1950 its trade surplus with Britain stood at $68 million as compared to $457 million just four years earlier.[2]

World War II saw the transformation of the United States into a major importer of ores, concentrates and basic metals. Canadian reserves were the logical and secure way to meet American needs. In 1948, the United States imported 60 per cent more lead and zinc from Canada than it did annually from 1937 to 1939. By 1957, metal's and mineral's share of Canadian exports across the 49th parallel had approximately doubled, reaching 35 per cent, and the U.S. share of Canadian exports jumped to 60 per cent.[3]

Foreign, mostly American, investors poured $1.4 billion into Canadian mining and smelting industries from 1945 to 1955.[4] Foreign control of these activities rose from 42 per cent in 1939 to nearly 60 per cent in the mid-1950s.[5]

U.S. and Canadian policies were important in this process. The U.S. tariff that emerged from early rounds of negotiations sponsored by the General Agreement on Tariffs and Trade (GATT) was characterized by higher rates of duty on manufactures than on natural resource products. Canada's decision not to enter into a free trade agreement in 1948 caused the continuation of high levels of protection for manufacturing. Together, these policies discouraged the rationalization of Canadian industry, constrained the growth of intraindustry trade in manufactures, and essentially required that Canada replace its lost trade surplus with Britain with more resource-based exports and capital inflows. Granatstein, writing about Mackenzie King's rejection of free trade, observed:

> ... the process of continental integration proceeded all the same, under both King and his successor, Louis St. Laurent. The shortage of American dollars was perennial, and the integrative effects of Hyde Park and the 1947 [Marshall Plan] agreements were clear. To get dollars, the Canadian government actively encouraged American investment. And the United States, concerned about its diminishing stocks of strategic metals and minerals ... looked eagerly to Canada. The result was a massive inflow of American development capital ... and the great Canadian economic boom.[6]

By 1960, though, the metals and minerals boom had subsided. Prior to that date, real growth in resource extraction actually outpaced resource processing and secondary manufacturing. Although the rents accruing from mining were to remain substantial for many years, and tight global supplies and price bubbles for most resources in 1972-74 and for petroleum in the late 1970s briefly increased these rents, these industries never again led Canadian growth.

Manufacturing Moves to Centre Stage

The next great impetus to bilateral trade and investment came in the automobile industry. As with mining, smelting, and basic metals, changes both in objective economic conditions and government policies played a role.

During the 1950s and early 1960s, the scope for economies of scale in automotive design and production greatly widened, and eventually only four major North American producers survived. As making cars and trucks in Canada for the domestic market became increasingly unattractive, even behind a 17.5 per cent tariff, Ottawa initiated a duty remission program to encourage exports to the United States in 1962 and 1963. A countervailing duty suit brought by an injured U.S. radiator manufacturer resulted in a Treasury finding of an export subsidy, and the inevitability of countervailing duties precipitated negotiation of the Automotive Agreement of 1965.[7]

The agreement resulted in the rationalization of production on a continental basis, dramatic improvements in Canadian productivity and wages,[8] and massive growth in intraindustry trade—automotive product's share of Canadian exports jumped from less than one per cent in 1960 to more than 30 per cent in the 1970s.

Also significant, the 1960s and 1970s witnessed a major increase in exports of non-automotive secondary manufactures—their share nearly doubled. This reflected improving Canadian comparative advantages in some secondary manufactures as the margins of Canadian advantages in resource products declined.

Table 1
Canadian Exports to the United States

	1960 %	1970 %	1980 %
Motor Vehicles and Parts	*	31	22
Other Secondary Manufactures	12	18	22
Metals and Minerals	28	16	16
Petroleum and Natural Gas	4	8	15
Forest Products	43	19	17
Farm and Fish Products	10	5	3
Chemicals and Fertilizer	3	3	5

* = less than 0.5 per cent

Source: Peter Morici, "U.S.-Canadian Trade Relations in the 1980s," *The American Review of Canadian Studies*, Vol. XV, No. 3, (Summer 1987), p. 165.

Canadian Policy in the 1960s and 1970s

Changing Attitudes

In the 1960s and 1970s, several internal and external factors caused a gradual re-evaluation of Canada's basic approaches to economic development and industrial policy.

First, the formation of the European Community and the European Free Trade Association, the rapid economic progress that followed, and the gains accruing to Canadians under the Automotive Agreement made it apparent that other Canadian manufacturers could greatly improve their competitiveness if given free and secure access to a larger market. In this context, Canada's trading relationship with the United States again attracted considerable attention among private-sector leaders, academics and public officials as evidenced by the publication of R.J. and Paul Wonnacott's classic study in 1967, the attention paid to the issue by the Canadian-American Committee in the mid-1960s, and by the publications of the Economic Council of Canada in the 1970s.[9]

Second, as the resource boom subsided and Canadian growth slowed, the importance of improving manufacturing productivity became more apparent. Although Canadian manufacturers substantially reduced the U.S. productivity advantage in the 1950s and 1960s, progress slowed in the 1970s and a substantial gap remained. Also, Canadian progress consistently lagged behind Japan, Germany and France.[10]

Third, the emergence of Japan and then the newly industrializing countries in Asia and Latin America as major exporters in a succession of mature industries made even more obvious the need to raise productivity.

Fourth, with regard to manufacturing, several structural issues attracted attention: the amount of value added Canadian resources received before being exported; the "truncated" nature of much of Canada's manufacturing;[11] Canada's weakness in technology-intensive manufacturing and low rank among industrial countries in R&D spending.

Fifth, large multinational corporations (MNCs) in Canada were perceived by some Canadians as exerting too much influence over: the location and structure of production; the character and content of trade; the scope of business activities—e.g., product development, strategic planning and exporting—undertaken in Canada; the quality of employment opportunities available to Canadians. Whether a high degree of foreign ownership and control best served Canada's national interests emerged as a major public policy issue.

Sixth, persistent disparities in income and employment opportunities among Canada's regions—i.e., lagging progress in Quebec and the Atlantic provinces—became increasingly recognized as a critical public policy question. Moreover, policy makers became increasingly aware that the entrance of the baby boom cohort into the labour force would strain the economy's capacity to create the necessary number and quality of jobs.

Seventh, these economic issues were further complicated by growing anxiety that the U.S.-Canadian economic integration was fostering social and cultural integration. Speaking of growing bilateral commercial ties, the 1970 Canadian White Paper on Foreign Policy stated that:

> while such developments should be beneficial for Canada's economic growth, the constant danger that sovereignty, independence and cultural identity may be impaired will require a conscious effort on Canada's part to keep the whole situation under control.[12]

By the early 1970s, Canadians found themselves in a rather ambivalent situation. Economic efficiency could be substantially increased through further integration with the U.S. economy, notably through the elimination of tariffs and an open door to American capital and technology. However, U.S. international, industrial and political leadership were slipping, raising questions about the consequences for U.S. policy towards Canada.[13] Further economic integration, under prevailing arrangements, could only raise the influence of U.S. MNCs on Canada's economic structure and of American media and social and political institutions on Canada's national life.

Eighth, and not least, a number of U.S. actions helped motivate more independent/nationalistic Canadian foreign, economic and cultural policies. For example, Canadians resented the extraterritorial application of U.S. law on subsidiaries operating outside the United States.[14] Also in the late 1960s, the Johnson Administration avoided reconciling the competing fiscal demands created by its Great Society programs and the Vietnam war. This ultimately set off a costly inflation spiral and, more immediately, precipitated balance of payments difficulties and several unilateral U.S. actions to stem capital outflows.

In 1971, the U.S. government began permitting U.S. companies to establish Domestic International Sales Corporations (DISCs) to bolster exports.[15] More significantly, the United States shocked the financial world by taking the dollar off the gold standard and imposing a 10 per cent across-the-board import surcharge. The Nixon Administration refused to grant Canada special exemption from either the effects of DISCs or the import surcharge. This American stance stood in sharp contrast to earlier Canadian requests for special treatment regarding U.S. balance of payments measures in the 1960s and U.S. treatment of Canadian exports under Lend-Lease, the Marshall Plan and even U.S. loans to Britain in World War I.

Also, as discussed in Chapter 1 and below, U.S. trade policy in the 1970s became increasingly defined by private actions through safeguard and countervailing duty suits. As it emerged, this reliance on contingent protection was seen as depriving competitive Canadian producers of the benefits anticipated from GATT-sponsored, reciprocal tariff reductions.

When the Trudeau government sought exemption for Canada from the import surcharge, the United States refused. President Nixon articulated the view that the United States and its allies should be free to formulate policies that served their sovereign and sometimes divergent interests. In an April 1972 speech before parliament he stated:

> ...each nation must define the nature of its own interests; each nation must decide the requirements of its own security; each nation must determine the path of its own progress. What we seek is a policy which enables us to share international responsibilities in a spirit of international partnership. We believe that the spirit of partnership is strongest when partners are self reliant.[16]

While relieving the United States of the burden of special status for Canada, Nixon also acknowledged Canada's right to pursue its own economic course.

No self-respecting nation can or should accept the proposition that it should always be economically dependent upon any other nation. Let us recognize for once and for all that the only basis for a sound and healthy relationship between our two proud peoples is to find a pattern of economic interaction which is beneficial to both our countries and which respects Canada's right to chart its own economic course.[17]

This marked the end of the special relationship. The Third Option paper (discussed below) came on the heels of these U.S. actions and a generally tougher U.S. stance on bilateral commercial issues.

Together, these trends generated enormous impetus for actions and institutional changes intended to improve the functioning of the Canadian economy, foster industrial adjustments and to establish more proactive economic and cultural policies that would assert Canadian independence in the context of growing bilateral trade and investment.

Trade and Investment Policies

Canada participated fully in the item-by-item tariff cuts negotiated in the first five GATT rounds from 1947 to 1962. However, in the Kennedy Round (1968-1972), Canada declined to participate in the linear tariff reductions agreed to by the United States and the EC. Owing to concerns about the ability of its overdiversified industries to adjust as easily as those of other countries, it accepted fewer and smaller tariff cuts.

In 1972, Secretary of State for External Affairs, Mitchell Sharp, proposed the Third Option, a policy of diversifying Canada's commercial relationship by placing more emphasis on Europe and other trading partners.[18] Ultimately, a two-track approach to policy emerged. Canada would reassert its commitment to trade liberalization under the GATT through full participation in Tokyo Round tariff reductions. It also developed other industrial policies aimed at influencing patterns of resource allocation, production and trade.[19] In addition, it took trade actions in cultural industries, which increased support for Canadian media and precipitated disputes with the United States.[20]

Turning to foreign investment policies, sentiment grew that foreign subsidiaries should be encouraged or required to operate in ways perceived to be more consistent with Canadian industrial development aspirations.[21] Concern about the conduct of foreign subsidiaries was understandable considering that by 1963 foreign control in mining and smelting had risen to 60 per cent. In petroleum and manufacturing it stood at 84 and 60 per cent respectively.[22] Within manufacturing, foreign ownership was particularly significant in rubber, automotive products, other transportation equipment, agricultural machinery, electrical equipment, and chemicals.[23]

The 1957 Gordon Royal Commission Report expressed some anxiety about the potential for conflict between the interests of Canadians and parent companies of foreign subsidiaries. The first broad action came in 1966, when Minister of Trade and Commerce Robert Winters circulated voluntary guidelines to 3,500 foreign subsidiaries.

In 1968, the Watkins Task Force[24] recommended making the 1966 guidelines mandatory and creating a government agency to administer them. With regard to increasing Canadian ownership, the principal recommendation implemented was the creation of the Canadian Development Corporation in 1971 (discussed below).

In 1972, the Gray Task Force Report[25] focused on the effects of foreign ownership and control on the structure of Canadian industry. It introduced the concept of "truncation," holding that MNCs with subsidiaries in Canada tended to undertake desirable corporate functions such as R & D in their home countries. The report proposed establishing an administrative review of designated categories of foreign investment. In 1973 the Trudeau government created the Foreign Investment Review Agency (FIRA). From April 1974 until it was replaced by Investment Canada in 1985, FIRA screened most foreign acquisitions, and from October 1975, foreign plans to establish new businesses in Canada. FIRA assessed projects on the basis of "significant benefits to Canada." Among the critical criteria applied were compatibility with national industrial policies, increased Canadian employment, increased resource processing and purchase of Canadian goods and services (import substitution), and additional exports.[26]

Other Industrial Policies

During the 1960s and 1970s, federal and provincial governments increasingly used non-tariff devices to maintain or create employment in depressed communities, promote adjustment in mature industries, and seed the development of technology-intensive activities. Among these tools were:

- technical assistance and extensive financial incentives in the form of grants and low-interest loans to industry;
- the aggressive use of government procurement;
- efforts to steer private procurement for major resource projects to Canadian suppliers;
- duty remission programs to encourage foreign manufacturers to source components or locate plants in Canada.[27]

Also, public ownership expanded in the resource and manufacturing sectors—e.g., steel, pulp and paper, petroleum and natural gas. In 1976, Petro-Canada was established to facilitate a greater Canadian presence in the energy sector. The Canadian Development Corporation was created as a quasi-public/private company to encourage the development and maintenance of Canadian-owned and controlled firms. The CDC's mandate in selecting investments included emphasis on technology-intensive activities and those with good potential for exports.[28] By the early 1980s, the CDC had investments in petrochemicals, mining, oil and gas, health care industries, electronics, fishing, and industrial automation. It had become an important actor in the creation of new enterprises, amassing the largest pool of venture capital in Canada.

Tensions and Consensus: The Means and Goals of Canadian Policy

By the time Pierre Trudeau had completed his third mandate in June 1979, Canada had erected a rather substantial array of policies including a wide range of financial incentives and performance reviews for new foreign investment, which could be and often were used to influence indigenous Canadian firms and foreign subsidiaries reactions to new market challenges and opportunities. To some extent, these reflected Canada's need, like those of other industrialized countries, to cope with a changing international global competitive environment.[29]

These industrial policies had a pronounced nationalist impulse, reflecting the view that Canada's industrial structure should not be determined entirely by market forces and corporate management decisions that were often inward-looking or heavily influenced by the home offices of foreign MNCs.

During the 1970s, though, the nationalists' position had not reached true ascendancy. The Trudeau governments of that decade did not embrace a broad *dirigiste* approach to policy with an explicit statement of goals and strategy. Policy remained a mixture of internationalist and nationalist approaches. Canada participated in the Tokyo Round talks that would substantially lower the protection afforded manufacturing, while it implemented policies to prepare for and manage industrial adjustment.

These industrial policies did reflect some consistent themes and some consensus among Canadians about the goals of policy, if not an agreement about appropriate means. These implicit objectives included:

- rationalization to improve productivity in manufacturing;
- more R & D and emphasis on technology-intensive activities;
- increased national benefits from resource development;
- better regional balance in incomes and employment opportunities;
- greater Canadian ownership and control over the means of production, especially in the resource sector.[30]

American Responses to Canadian Policies in the 1960s and 1970s

The buildup of Canadian industrial incentives and regional aids were, at various times, the focus of intense American scrutiny, which in turn exposed the vulnerability of Canadian industrial policies to American reactions. The two areas that generated the most heat in the 1980s—subsidies and foreign investment policies—engendered quite different U.S. responses during the 1960s and 1970s.

Regarding subsidies, American reactions in the 1960s and 1970s illustrate how private initiatives—suits brought under U.S. trade remedy laws—played an increasing role in precipitating change and in some cases defining U.S. policy.

As previously noted, when Canada offered duty remission benefits on auto parts exports in 1962 and 1963, a U.S. radiator manufacturer sought countervailing duties. Following an affirmative finding by the Treasury Department, the inevitability of U.S. countervailing duties precipitated the Automotive Agreement.[31]

In 1973, the United States broadened its concept of countervailable export assistance to include domestic production subsidies when countervailing duties were levied on tires imported from a Michelin factory in Nova Scotia that had benefitted from a regional development grant and other Department of Regional Economic Expansion assistance.[32] During the 1970s other countervailing duty suits were initiated. However, the United States agreed to waive duties for the duration the Tokyo Round (1973-79).[33] Hence, the effects of these suits were generally limited to arousing Canadian sensitivities to the growing importance of subsidies in the minds of the U.S. trade policy community, and the threat which the evolving U.S. system of contingent protection posed to independent Canadian industrial and regional development policies.

In 1978, Canada granted Volkswagen a duty remission order giving benefits for parts purchased and exported from Canada, including components sent to the United States. The United States protested strongly. Subsequent duty remission agreements with foreign automakers did not provide credit for exports to the United States until the Mulroney government again began granting such credit just prior to the Quebec Summit in March 1985.

In 1979, the United States once again broadened its concept of countervailable subsidies—this time to include R & D aids. The Commerce Department found a Canadian R & D grant for the development of a Liquid Optic Level Sensing Device to be countervailable, arguing the aid was given after a patent had been awarded and was therefore deemed a product development grant.[34] By the late 1970s, the Canadian-American Committee concluded that subsidies and countervailing duties had become the most sensitive non-tariff trade issue.[35]

The U.S. response to FIRA was less assertive. By the mid-1970s, the imposition of screening coupled with the nationalist rhetoric caused American investors to feel less welcome in Canada and to become concerned about the potential for increased discrimination.[36] However, FIRA's trade-related performance requirements did not precipitate a strong U.S. response until the 1980s.

Looking across the array of Canadian industrial policies of the 1970s and American responses, it appears that U.S. policy makers were willing to accept Canadian aspirations to diversify international commercial relations, exert more control over foreign investment, forge a more proactive industrial policy, and assert its cultural sovereignty, although they viewed these initiatives with some puzzlement and growing concern. Where American interests were irritated, the U.S. government resisted pressures for sweeping retaliation and stressed consultation.[37] Where U.S. firms or workers could establish specific grievance or injury under U.S. trade remedy laws, Washington took action.

The U.S. government tried to resist pressures to link issues. For example, although U.S. border broadcasters were briefly able to link their problem to an unrelated tax issue (see footnote 20), Washington ultimately denied them strong unrelated retaliation; instead, the Congress passed mirror legislation in 1984.[38]

In this context, the private sector became increasingly assertive in the use of subsidies law, as described above, safeguard actions and grey-area measures,[39] and other trade remedy laws. In this way, the influence of private actions on the direction of trade policy grew.

The Ascent of Canadian Nationalism

In 1979, Joe Clark was elected on a conservative, pro-business platform, and his election appeared to signal the decline of nationalist policies. Lasting only nine months, his government's impact on industrial policy was minimal.

In the 1980 election, the Liberal Party platform gave top priority to energy policy and industrial strategy. Trudeau also promised to expand FIRA's activities.[40] When the Liberals returned to office in March 1980, many policy makers were optimistic that the rents from Canada's considerable resource wealth could finance an aggressive industrial policy that could catapult Canadian industry into a more competitive future.

The National Energy Program (NEP) was unveiled in October, 1980 with the stated goals of:

- *security* from import-supply disruptions;
- *fairness* in pricing (i.e., domestic prices lower than world prices) and in revenue sharing (i.e., more money for Ottawa in the split among the energy companies, the producing provinces and the federal government);
- *increased Canadian opportunities* in the energy sector (i.e., increased domestic ownership and the industrial benefits that could flow from procurement).[41]

While defining specific actions to achieve these ends, the NEP was also a critical component of a broader set of initiatives in the areas of foreign investment, industrial and R & D incentives, and procurement.

Foreign Investment

Under Minister for Industry, Trade and Commerce Herb Gray, FIRA adopted a tougher stance towards proposed new foreign investments, seeking more commitments for Canadian procurement, R & D and the like. Many applications were withdrawn or never formally submitted because FIRA's demands seemed severe.[42] In April 1980, the government announced its intention to expand the FIRA mandate to review of the operations of *established* foreign subsidiaries. This would have opened the door to import-substitution, export, investment, R & D, and other similar requirements on nearly 40 per cent of Canadian manufacturing and over 45 per cent of Canadian mining.[43]

Also the NEP contained specific policies to increase Canadian ownership. Among these were a 25 per cent Crown interest on new oil and gas development on Canada Lands which applied to leases obtained and priced before the NEP was announced. Other new policies under the NEP included changes in the tax treatment of exploration and development costs that discriminated against foreign firms, mandatory Canadian private-sector participation in oil and gas development on Canada Lands, and an excise tax to finance Petro-Canada's acquisition of one or two foreign subsidiaries.

Industrial Incentives

As presented with the 1980 and 1981 budgets, a critical element of the NEP was to increase Ottawa's share of the revenues generated by petroleum production from 10 to 25 per cent. Much of these new revenues were to be used for industrial and regional development programs.[44] Prior to these announcements, Herb Gray had advocated in cabinet the aggressive use of subsidies and tighter controls on foreign investments as part of a broader industrial strategy to encourage high-technology activities and industrial adjustment. Also, in January 1981, the Ministry of State for Science and Technology published *R & D Policies, Planning and Programming*, which stated the government's aspiration to increase Canadian R & D spending from 1.0 to 1.5 per cent of GNP, in part by leveraging private resources.[45] Further, in the automotive sector, duty remissions were granted to Asian and European vehicle producers in return for purchasing Canadian parts for export to countries other than the United States—e.g., the Honda duty remission order of August 13, 1980.[46] Finally, Ottawa bailed out Massey-Ferguson and turned over its own highly profitable 48 per cent holding in the CDC to the new Canadian Development Investment Corporation, permitting the federal government's share of CDC profits to cover losing investments in Canadair and deHavilland.[47]

Public and Private Procurement

Great emphasis was placed on creating a broader domestic market for indigenous high-technology firms through public procurement and by encouraging private firms to buy Canadian products. In March 1980, the federal government established the *Procurement Review Mechanism*. Its objectives were to use federal procurement to achieve lasting benefits in the electronics and other high-technology sectors, stimulate new product innovation and improve opportunities for small businesses, particularly in depressed regions. Undertakings to purchase Canadian products were important for winning approval in more rigorous FIRA reviews. Further, as originally proposed, the NEP announced "strict requirements for use of Canadian goods and services in exploration, development and production programs on the Canadian Lands, and in major non-conventional oil projects."[48] Policy makers became interested in extending this approach to other "mega projects" and to procurement generally in the mining and minerals processing sectors.

U.S. Responses to Canadian Nationalism

The NEP and a more vigorous FIRA attracted a strong U.S. response for several reasons.[49] First, several NEP provisions for achieving greater Canadian ownership were viewed by Washington as violating international principles of national treatment for foreign investors; some were seen as unfairly retroactive, especially the 25 per cent Crown interest on Canada Lands. With respect to procurement, Americans believed the NEP violated the GATT. Second, just as Canada was seeking to buy back substantial amounts of its petroleum industry and FIRA was taking a much tougher stand in reviews of U.S. firms' investment proposals, several Canadian firms attempted unfriendly takeovers of American companies. Third, tougher reviews of new foreign investments raised questions about the legality under the GATT of FIRA efforts to obtain undertakings regarding domestic sourcing and exports. U.S. government responses to the NEP and FIRA proceeded along three avenues—bilateral consultations, threats of unilateral retaliation, and multilateral actions.

Starting in late 1980, U.S. and Canadian officials had a series of meetings. U.S. officials came seeking major changes in the NEP, while Canadians saw these meetings as opportunities to explain the rationale for their policies. In May 1981, Canada did change the NEP's procurement language to conform with the GATT and offered *ex gratia* payments for its 25 per cent Crown interests in new developments on Canada Lands.

In 1981 and early 1982, Washington contemplated various retaliatory actions, including denying Canadian firms leases on

U.S. federal lands under the *Minerals Lands Leasing Act of 1920*. Canada, it was argued, could be declared a nonreciprocating country under the act because it denied "similar or like" privileges to U.S. citizens and companies under NEP. Some congressmen pressured Secretary of Interior James Watt to so act but he resisted. As tensions grew, the environment became unusually heated for Canadian-American diplomacy, and there were caustic statements from both sides.[50]

In the end, Washington could not frame actions that were not as damaging to its interests as those of Ottawa and declined meaningful retaliation.[51] By mid-1982, both governments recognized the need to manage their disputes in a less hostile and quieter manner and made public statements downplaying irritants.

The United States adopted the posture that the economic costs of maintaining the NEP and lost foreign investment would ultimately cause Canada to reconsider its nationalist policies. In the meantime, the United States pressed its case in multilateral forums. The GATT ultimately found that FIRA's domestic sourcing requirements violated Article III(4); Canada agreed to change this practice but declined to rule on export requirements.

In November 1981, the Trudeau government postponed plans to extend FIRA's reach to the activities of established foreign subsidiaries, and stated that tactics employed in the NEP to increase Canadian ownership in the energy sector would not be generalized to other sectors. In September 1982, Edward Lumley replaced Herb Gray as the minister responsible for FIRA. Reflecting the new tone of the government, Canada began actively seeking foreign investment. With respect to the NEP, Ottawa held its ground. It made some minor concessions, but major changes would come with the government of Prime Minister Mulroney.

By 1983, U.S. policy had returned to a more normal course. The emphasis was again on raising issues such as those relating to the NEP and other trade and investment irritants in bilateral meetings and multilateral fora, and on asserting U.S. rights under the GATT through the application of U.S. trade remedy laws when U.S. business and labour interests were directly affected by Canadian policies. This policy, quite reminiscent of the 1970s, nevertheless was increasingly troubling to Canadians because of exceedingly aggressive U.S. application of trade remedy laws, especially subsidy/countervailing duty provisions. Canada, for its part, continued to offer industrial and regional development aids, although their use was substantially curtailed.

Origins of the Free Trade Agreement

During the final Trudeau years, as the outlook for Canada's important resource sector weakened and unemployment remained well above U.S. levels, enthusiasm for nationalist policies waned and the nature of Canada's fundamental economic problems became more widely understood. Interventionist policies had failed to make manufacturing more competitive. As international oil prices levelled off and then declined, the inherent contradictions in the NEP's pricing policies and the large costs of Canadianization became more apparent. FIRA and the NEP drove away foreign investors in non-energy areas where Canada sorely needed their capital and expertise.

Focusing on metals and minerals, the 1982-83 recession hit these industries very hard, especially steel and nonferrous metals in both the United States and Canada. There was growing recognition that new technologies, substitute materials and the downsizing of automobiles were reducing demand for important Canadian exports (e.g., steel, copper, zinc, nickel, and lead) and that new developing-countries' suppliers had permanently reduced market shares for many Canadian companies. From 1981 until after the free trade negotiations began in 1986, Canadian exporters endured slow growing volumes and flat or declining prices.[52]

Among Canada's resource exports, only forest products kept pace with the general rate of increase in prices among all industrial products (see Appendix Table A1). With most American resource producers facing similar problems, protectionist sentiments in the Congress posed the persistent threat of lost access to the critical U.S. market. The United States took trade actions in potash, steel, softwood lumber and specialty steel, and the threat of actions in nonferrous metals was apparent.

Macroeconomic conditions exacerbated the effects of these trends. As U.S. budget deficits and capital inflows rose during the early 1980s, the U.S. dollar rose against the yen and European currencies. Although the Canadian dollar fell somewhat against the U.S. dollar, it followed the U.S. dollar up against offshore currencies, damaging prospects for resource exports to European and other third country markets.[53]

Turning to secondary manufacturing, Canadian productivity growth lagged behind progress in the United States. The progress towards reducing the U.S. advantages achieved in the 1970s stalled in the 1980s.

Table 2
Estimated Output per Hour in Manufacturing*

	1950	1960	1970	1980	1988
United States	100	100	100	100	100
Canada	52	63	72	75	70
Japan	11	22	47	76	86
Germany	34	58	78	93	88
France	29	39	56	71	68
Italy	23	29	45	63	63
United Kingdom	33	34	37	37	41

* Daly and MacCharles developed estimates of relative productivity levels among industrialized countries. From three base studies, they established productivity comparisons for 1977 among the United States, Japan and Canada; for 1980 among the United States and among the four European countries shown here. These were in turn extended back to 1950 and forward to 1984 using Bureau of Labour Statistics estimates of annual changes in labour productivity in each country. Such estimates while having their limitations (discussed by Daly and MacCharles) are not affected by changes in exchange rates. These data were in turn extended by the present author using the same BLS data series through 1988.

Sources: D.J. Daly and D.C, MacCharles, *Focus on Real Wages* (Vancouver: The Fraser Institute, 1986), Appendix A; Peter Morici, *Meeting the Competitive Challenge*, p. 13; Bureau of Labour Statistics.

As the 1980s unfolded, Canadian automotive exports revived and were greatly aided by the U.S. voluntary restraint agreements with Japan, but other secondary manufactures' share of exports ceased climbing until the free trade negotiations were well underway in 1987.

Table 3
Canadian Exports to the United States

	1970 %	1980 %	1981 %	1983 %	1985 %	1987 %
Motor Vehicles and Parts	31	22	23	33	36	36
Other Secondary Manufactures	18	22	25	22	21	24
Metals and Minerals	24	16	15	11	11	8
Petroleum and Natural Gas	8	15	13	11	9	8
Forest Products	19	17	16	15	11	8
Farm and Fish Products	5	3	3	4	4	4
Chemicals and Fertilizer	3	5	5	4	4	4

Source: Peter Morici, "U.S.-Canadian Trade Relations in the 1980s," *The American View of Canadian Studies*, Vol. XVII, No. 2, (Summer 1987), pp. 165 and author's estimates.

Concerns grew about whether Canadian manufacturing was adjusting rapidly enough to the new opportunities and to competition created by Tokyo Round tariff reductions (1980-87) plus expanding industrial capabilities in East Asia. Mounting protectionist pressures and actions in the United States, and the escalating threat of U.S. countervailing and antidumping duties, which could at any time close the U.S. market to competitive Canadian manufacturers, were seen as major impediments to investment and rationalization in Canadian manufacturing. In a nutshell, tariff cuts had exposed Canadian manufacturing to more Asian and American competition, but the threat of U.S. contingent protection blocked Canadians from taking full advantage of their largest potential market.

Canadians began to examine alternative strategies to improve economic performance. In August 1983, the Canadian *Trade Policy Review* acknowledged the potential benefits to

Canadian manufacturing of better access to the U.S. market and suggested a series of sectoral arrangements.[54] Preliminary talks followed in early 1984,[55] although the Reagan Administration privately indicated to Canadian officials flexibility in the scope and types of agreements that could be achieved.[56]

For the Reagan Administration, these talks represented opportunities at both the multilateral and bilateral levels. Frustrated by the pace of progress in the GATT and faced by criticism abroad of unilateralism due to its now quite frequent resort to contingent protection, negotiations with Canada, at least as viewed from the Potomac, provided the opportunity for the United States to demonstrate its approach to international trade. It was willing to liberalize trade with countries interested in opening their markets and was quite prepared to walk the bilateral road if its aspirations for progress in the GATT were frustrated. Equally important, talks with Canada provided the opportunity to establish rules regarding investment, energy and services, and to achieve some understanding with Canada about subsidies. Such objectives would be best served by a comprehensive agreement.

U.S. officials privately admitted scepticism about the prospects of negotiating sectoral agreements, owing to the difficulties of achieving a balanced package and one that Congress would approve. However, cautious of arousing Canadian nationalists, U.S. officials avoided taking the lead in suggesting a comprehensive free trade agreement. In any case, formal negotiations awaited the outcome of fall 1984 elections in both countries.

At the March 18, 1985 Quebec City Summit, President Ronald Reagan and Prime Minister Brian Mulroney agreed to assign highest priority to finding ways to reduce existing barriers to trade and facilitate trade and investment flows. Subsequently, Canada's trade minister undertook cross-country consultations to gauge national sentiment about and build support for a free trade agreement with the United States. Several private groups including the prestigious Canadian-American Committee and the Business Council on National Issues endorsed the concept. A critical report by advocates Richard Lipsey and Murray Smith captured much public attention by making a clear and compelling case for free trade.[57]

In September 1985, the Macdonald Royal Commission,[58] as anticipated, recommended that Canada give high priority to negotiating a comprehensive free trade arrangement with the United States. The Canadian Minister for International Trade, James Kelleher, and his American counterpart, Clayton Yeutter, endorsed the idea in independent reports to the prime minister and the president, and Brian Mulroney asked President Reagan to undertake comprehensive negotiations.

As Donald Macdonald, of the Royal Commission, testified before Congress a year later, the Canadian decision to seek free trade was inspired by the conviction that Canada could no longer depend on natural resource exports to propel growth. It must become more competitive in world markets in manufactured goods and services, and hence it must restructure substantially to achieve this end.[59] Non-tariff barriers and their threat—namely the U.S. system of contingent protection—were identified as a major obstacle to investment in Canada and restructuring:

> This latter conclusion has been reinforced during the course of the past twelve months in which Canadians have seen a range of Canadian products sold into the American market faced with actual or proposed import restrictions as a result of countervailing duty or safeguard actions involving softwood lumber, shakes and shingles, steel, groundfish . . . and a range of other agricultural and natural resource products.[60]

Once again, a reassessment of Canada's export prospects, the constraints imposed by market size on its manufacturing sector and a shift in U.S. trade policy caused Canadians to reassess the costs and benefits of seeking further economic integration with the United States. It should be recognized that Canadian longstanding concerns about cultural and economic sovereignty have not evaporated. This is why Canada negotiated hard for the exclusion of cultural industries from most provisions of the free trade agreement and for a U.S. acknowledgement of Canada's *right* to screen direct foreign acquisitions of its largest industrial companies.

Notes

1. Reuber, *The Growth and Changing Composition of Trade between the United States and Canada*, p. 136.

2. Cuff and Granatstein, *American Dollars—Canadian Prosperity*, p. 136.

3. *Ibid.*

4. *Ibid.*, p. 143.

5. Brecher and Reisman, *Canada-U.S. Economic Relations*, p. 101.

6. J.L. Granatstein, "The Course of Canadian-American Relations since 1945" in Charles F. Doran and John F. Sigler (eds.), *Canada and the United States: Enduring Friendship, Persistent Stress* (Englewood Cliffs, N.J.: Prentice Hall, Inc., 1985), p. 50.

7. Essentially, under the agreement, the United States admits duty-free Canadian-made products having 50 per cent U.S./Canadian content. Canada admits duty-free vehicles and original equipment parts made by firms that assemble one car in Canada for each car sold there and achieve value-added in Canada equal to 60 per cent of sales there. Among passenger car makers, only General Motors, Ford, Chrysler, and Volvo meet these conditions.
   By meeting Canada's strict content requirements (often called safeguards), General Motors, Chrysler, Ford, and Volvo may bring their "captive" imports into Canada without paying a 9.2 per cent duty—a decided advantage over Japanese, Korean and other foreign companies.
   Until European and Asian imports captured major shares of the North American market, the safeguards substantially tied production to sales in Canada. When Volkswagen and Asian manufacturers began establishing plants in the United States, partly in response to U.S. protectionist pressures, Canada offered duty remission on their vehicle imports in return for purchasing Canadian parts for export or for establishing significant production facilities in Canada. This importantly shifted the incentives for foreign manufacturers as to the choice of plant locations between the two countries in favour of Canada.
   The FTA is phasing out tariffs on bilateral trade in *all* automotive products (including replacement parts and the U.S./Canadian products of Asian and European companies) that meet or exceed a 50 per cent U.S./Canadian direct-cost-of-processing requirement. Unlike the old U.S. 50 per cent North American value-added rule, overhead and other indirect costs may not be counted. Under the FTA, Canada also agrees to phase out duty remission benefits; the three major North American manufacturers and Volvo may continue to meet the old Canadian production requirements if they wish to bring captive imports into Canada duty-free. Canada also

agrees not to extend the latter benefits to other foreign passenger vehicle manufacturers.

8. Prior to 1965, Canadian wages were about 30 percent lower than U.S. wages.

9. See Paul and R.J. Wonnacott, *Free Trade Between the United States and Canada: The Possible Economic Effects* (Cambridge, Mass.: Harvard University Press, 1967); Sperry Lea, *A Canada-U.S. Free-Trade Arrangement: A Survey of Possible Characteristics* (Montreal: Canadian-American Committee, 1963); *A Possible Plan for a U.S.-Canada Free Trade Area*—prepared by the staff of the Canadian-American Committee (Montreal, 1965); Economic Council of Canada, *Looking Outward* (Ottawa, 1975); Peyton V. Lyon, *Canada-United States Trade and Canadian Independence* (Ottawa: Economic Council of Canada, 1975).

10. See table 2 on p. 52.

11. Many foreign subsidiaries and indigenous firms were dependent on U.S. technology. They were oriented towards final fabrication or product assembly for sale only in Canada and exported less than their U.S. counterparts.

12. Canada Department of External Affairs, *Foreign Policy for Canadians* (Ottawa: 1970), p. 24.

13. Mitchell Sharp called attention to slipping U.S. industrial leadership in his "Third Option" paper. See "Canada-U.S. Relations: Options for the Future," *International Perspectives* (Autumn, 1972—special issue), pp. 1-24.

14. See Kingman Brewster, *Law and United States Business in Canada* (Montreal: Canadian American Committee, 1960) and Allan E. Gotlieb, "Extraterritoriality: The Canadian Perspective," Address before the New York Law Association (November 12, 1982).

15. The Revenue Act of 1971 permitted U.S. companies to establish and sell exports through DISCs as a means of sheltering export profits from taxation. In 1981, the GATT Council concluded DISC's tax benefits constituted an export subsidy and contravened U.S. obligations under Article XVI(4). See Peter Morici and Laura L. Megna, *U.S. Economic Policies Affecting Trade: A Quantitative Assessment* (Washington, D.C.: National Planning Association, 1983), pp. 83-84.

16. Lawrence Martin, *The Presidents and the Prime Ministers*, p. 251.

17. *Ibid.*, p. 252.

18. *Ibid.*

19. In retrospect, the Automotive Agreement was a precursor of this strategy. Through it, Canada sought the efficiencies that could be

obtained by reducing tariffs, while at the same time seeking to influence the patterns of investment, trade and bilateral specialization that would follow—in this case through performance requirements for foreign investors wishing to qualify for duty-free treatment.

20. Commercials were deleted from some U.S. television programs retransmitted on Canadian cable systems; these were replaced with Canadian advertising. Corporate income tax deductions were denied Canadian companies advertising in the Canadian edition of *Time* and several smaller periodicals. Commercial deletion was terminated. However, in early 1976, Canada instituted a policy of denying corporate tax deductions for advertising on U.S. border television stations with substantial audiences in Canada (Bill C-58).

21. The build-up of ideas leading to the creation of FIRA is discussed in more detail in Peter Morici, Arthur J.R. Smith, and Sperry Lea, *Canadian Industrial Policy* (Washington, D.C.: National Planning Association, 1981), pp. 36-41.

22. A.E. Safarian, *The Performance of Foreign-Owned Firms in Canada* (Montreal: Canadian-American Committee, 1969), p. xviii.

23. Morici, Smith, and Lea, *Canadian Industrial Policy*, p. 37.

24. Canada Task Force on the Structure of Canadian Industry [Melville H. Watkins, Head of Task Force] *Report* (Ottawa: Queen's Printer, 1968).

25. Canada, *Foreign Direct Investment in Canada* [Report prepared by Working Group under Hon. Herb Gray] (Ottawa: Information Canada, 1972).

26. Peter Morici, "U.S.-Canadian Trade Relations," in Peter Kresl (ed.), *Seen From the South* (Provo, Utah: Brigham Young University Press, 1989), pp. 97-99.

27. See Morici, Smith and Lea, *Canadian Industrial Policy* (1982), Chapter 4.

28. *Canada Yearbook 1978-79* (Ottawa: Statistics Canada, 1978), p. 883.

29. However, Canadian industry was facing more difficult adjustments than industry in other industrial countries owing to its historic orientation towards slower-growing, resource-based activities.

30. See Peter Morici "The Canada U.S.-Free Trade Agreement: Origins, Contents and Prospects," in Thomas Hyclak and Robert Thornton (eds.), *Economic Aspects of Regional Trading Agreements* (Brighton, England: Wheatsheaf, 1989) and Morici, Smith and Lea, *Canadian Industrial Policy*, Chapter 3.

31. An account of the events precipitating the Automotive Agreement may be found in "The Development of Canadian Policy Regarding Automotive Trade with the United States," in Morici, Smith and Lea, *Canadian Industrial Policy*, Appendix 1.

32. Gary Clyde Hufbauer, "Subsidy Issues After the Tokyo Round," in William R. Cline, *Trade Policy in the 1980s* (Washington, D.C.: Institute for International Economics, 1983), p. 352.

33. Murray Smith, *Bilateral Negotiations of Trade Laws: Possible Approaches* (Toronto: Canadian-American Committee, 1987), p. 21.

34. Hufbauer, *Trade Policies in the 1980s*, p. 354.

35. *Bilateral Relations in an Uncertain World Context: Canada-U.S. Relations in 1978*—prepared by the staff of the Canadian-American Committee (Montreal: 1978), p. 39.

36. *A Time of Difficult Transition: Canada-U.S. Relations in 1976*— prepared by the staff of the Canadian-American Committee (Montreal: 1976), p. 22.

37. *Ibid.*, p. 4.

38. See David Leyton-Brown, *Weathering the Storm: Canadian-U.S. Relations, 1980-83* (Toronto: Canadian-American Committee, 1985), pp. 62-66.

39. See Peter Morici and Laura L. Megna, *U.S. Economic Policies Affecting Trade: A Quantitative Assessment* (Washington: National Planning Association, 1983), pp. 14-30.

40. Stephen Clarkson, *Canada and the Reagan Challenge* (Ottawa: Canadian Institute for Economic Policy, 1982), p. 20.

41. Canada, Ministry of Energy, Mines and Resources, *The National Energy Program, 1980* (Ottawa: 1980).

42. Christopher Green, *Canadian Industrial Organization and Policy* (Toronto: McGraw-Hill Ryerson Ltd., 1985), p. 459.

43. Morici, Smith and Lea, *Canadian Industrial Policy*, p. 13.

44. *Ibid.*, pp. 48-49.

45. Canada Ministry of State for Science and Technology, *R & D Policies, Planning and Programming.* MOSST Background Paper 13 (Ottawa: January 1981).

46. Paul Wonnacott, *The United States and Canada: The Quest for Free Trade* (Washington, D.C.: Institute for International Economics, 1987), pp. 79-82.

47. Green, *Canadian Industrial Organization and Policy*, pp. 352-354.

48. Ministry of Energy, Mines and Resources, *The National Energy Program*, p. 103.

49. The following discussion of Canadian-American interactions during 1981 and 1982 draws from Leyton-Brown, *Weathering the Storm*, Chapter 3, and Edward Wonder, "The U.S. Response to the Canadian National Energy Program," *Canadian Public Policy*, Vol. III (Special Supplement, October 1982), pp. 480-493.

50. On September 22, 1981, U.S. Under Secretary of State Myer Rashish stated "sentiment [was] strong in favor of countermeasures against Canadian energy and investment policies. The dangers are real . . . ." On September 27, Marc Lalonde, Canadian Minister of Energy, Mines and Resources, said Mr. Rashish's statement was excessive, but that Canada would accept U.S. retaliation if that was the price for Canadianization of the oil and gas industry. See Leyton-Brown, *Weathering the Storm*, p. 39.

51. For example, declaring Canada a nonreciprocal country under the *Minerals Lands Leasing Act* would not have served U.S. objectives— forcing Canadian energy companies to redirect investment into Canada would only play into the hands of Canada's buy-back policy.

52. See Peter Morici, *The Global Competitive Struggle: Challenges to the United States and Canada* (Toronto: Canadian-American Committee, 1984), pp. 87-89, and Peter Morici, *Meeting the Competitive Challenge: Canada and the United States in the Global Economy* (Toronto: Canadian-American Committee, 1988), pp. 33-36.

53. See Morici, *Meeting the Competitive Challenge*, pp. 6-7.

54. Canada, Department of External Affairs, *A Review of Canadian Trade Policy: A Background Document to Canadian Trade Policy for the 1980s* (Ottawa: Minister of Supply and Services, 1983), pp. 209-212.

55. A joint work program was initiated in steel, urban mass transportation equipment, agricultural equipment and inputs (including chemicals), and computer services and informatics.

56. During the late 1970s, as the Tokyo Round was winding up, the U.S. government expressed interest in identifying additional ways to liberalize trade with Canada. The implementing legislation for the Tokyo Round directed the president to study the desirability of entering into trade agreements with other countries in the northern portion of the western hemisphere. The president concluded with regard to Canada that "further opportunities to rationalize industries through freer trade should be explored on both sides." See President of the United States [Ronald Reagan], "Report on North American Trade Agreements," (Washington, D.C.: U.S. Trade Representative, August 4, 1981), p. 3.

57. Richard G. Lipsey and Murray G. Smith, *Taking the Initiative: Canada's Trade Options* (Toronto: C.D. Howe Institute, 1985).

58. Canada, Royal Commission on the Economic Union and Development Prospects for Canada. [Macdonald Commission] *Report* (Ottawa, 1985).

59. See testimony of Donald S. Macdonald, in *United States/Canada Economic Relations*. Hearings before the Subcommittee on Economic Stabilization of the House Committee on Banking, Finance and Urban Affairs. 99 Cong. 2 sess. (Washington, D.C.: U.S. Government Printing Office, 1987), pp. 361-362.

60. *Ibid.*, pp, 362-363.

Chapter 3

The Free Trade Agreement

The election of Brian Mulroney in 1984 signaled a fundamental change in Canada's approach to U.S.-Canadian relations and industrial policy. The new Prime Minister cultivated closer ties with the Americans, jettisoned from Ottawa's power elite the ideology of economic nationalism, and reduced government involvement in economic development. Clearly, in both style and substance, the Mulroney government was more compatible with the conservative Reagan administration than its predecessor.

However, the 1984 election symbolized a turn in Canadian policy more than it marked one. In 1982, after the firestorm of protests from the Americans and from many quarters within Canada's business community, the Trudeau government began abandoning nationalist policies. This was symbolized perhaps most vividly by a change in leadership at the Foreign Investment Review Agency, which initiated an active campaign to attract foreign investors back to Canada. Ottawa also abandoned plans to extend National Energy Program-type policies—e.g., aggressive use of procurement and a reallocation of rents to promote industrial policy goals—to the mining and smelting sector. In addition, Canada began to explore ways to expand commerce and undertook sectoral trade negotiations with the United States.

Certainly, Mulroney extended this process by establishing a cordial relationship with President Reagan, reducing subsidies, privatizing many Crown corporations, dismantling important components of the National Energy Program, and ultimately, initiating the free trade negotiations.

Nevertheless, it is important to recognize that while many of the means of Canadian policy have changed, the goals remain remarkably stable. In the end, to be viewed a success in Canada, the Canada-U.S. Free Trade Agreement must be seen as serving Canada's long-term economic development objectives (e.g., improved productivity and competitiveness in manufacturing and increased Canadian participation in technology-intensive industries), while not compromising its nation-building goals (e.g., cultural and political sovereignty and better regional balance in economic opportunities). Canada's decision to negotiate and ratify the FTA reflected a conviction among its advocates that assured free access to the U.S. market is essential to modernizing and rationalizing manufacturing and that free trade could be achieved in such a way as not to compromise Canada's political and cultural institutions.

Canadian and U.S. Goals

Canada's officially stated goals in the bilateral negotiations were fourfold:

1. Canada sought to *enhance* its access to the U.S. market by eliminating tariffs and liberalizing non-tariff barriers. Among U.S. practices cited by Canadian officials were: discrimination in U.S. federal and state procurement, product standards, patents and copyrights.

2. Canada sought more *secure* access to the U.S. market by limiting the effects of U.S. trade remedy laws; it sought exemption from U.S. safeguard measures aimed at third countries and a clearer, bilaterally agreed upon, definition of a countervailable subsidy.

3. Canada sought to *enshrine* these gains through a strong agreement with an effective dispute settlement mechanism.

4. Canada wanted to *maintain policy discretion* in cultural industries and foreign investment, especially in some sensitive sectors.[1]

In addition, free trade was seen by many in Ottawa's policy elite as a way of reducing government intervention in the economy. Canadian negotiators expected to accept constraints on the use of domestic subsidies as part of a bilateral regime for applying countervailing duties, thereby limiting the role of subventions.

In the United States, free trade with Canada was seen as consistent with both its multilateral and bilateral goals. In the 1980s, the attention of U.S. trade policy makers increasingly focused on the limitations of General Agreement on Tariffs and Trade (GATT) treatment of agriculture, services and practices affecting market access for U.S. high-technology products—e.g., subsidies, trade-related investment policies, treatment of intellectual property rights, government procurement, and product standards. An agreement with Canada was regarded as possibly providing models for the GATT in several of these areas. Perhaps more importantly, the U.S. saw an agreement with Canada as providing a lever in the multilateral process by indicating to Japan, the European Community (EC) and others its preparedness to pursue bilateral and pluralateral avenues should the GATT process fail to deliver tangible benefits.[2]

Focusing on the bilateral relations, free trade offered the opportunity to eliminate higher Canadian tariffs[3] and to enshrine improvements in the trade and investment climate achieved during Prime Minister Trudeau's final years. Also, Canada had greatly loosened restrictions on energy exports to the United States and was again permitting some new U.S. investment in the oil and gas sector. The United States sought assurances that Canada would not again impose aggressive screening and performance requirements on U.S. investment or limit U.S. access to Canadian energy and other resources.

The United States sought controls on Canadian subsidies and elimination of duty remissions granted to foreign firms in exchange for exporting from or producing in Canada. Such benefits for Asian and European automakers were seen by Americans as compromising the Automotive Agreement of 1965. The United States also worked towards reduced discrimination in procurement and impediments to trade created by product standards and testing, a comprehensive agreement for business services, and improved market access in financial services.[4]

Essential Elements of the FTA[5]

The FTA makes important progress towards establishing fully integrated markets for goods, services and capital. It brings down many trade barriers, ensures that most others will not become more restrictive and establishes processes for reducing still others.

At its core, the agreement constitutes a political commitment to rely increasingly on jointly articulated rules for defining and enforcing the rights and protections afforded each country by GATT principles and to extend these rights and protections in a bilateral context.

By 1998, the FTA will eliminate tariffs,[6] duty drawbacks, and most import restrictions. It will prohibit export restrictions (unless grandfathered and except in periods of short supply),[7] export taxes and subsidies, and the dual pricing of exports.

For automotive products, bilateral trade will be duty free on products meeting a tough 50 per cent direct cost of processing rule. Unlike the old 50 per cent U.S./Canadian value-added rule applied by the United States under the Automotive Agreement, overhead and indirect costs will not count.[8] Canada is phasing out duty-remission benefits for Asian and European automakers that source parts in Canada for export or have established production facilities there.

Regarding safeguards, until 1998, tariffs may be restored for no more than three years should domestic producers suffer serious injury as a result of bilateral tariff reductions. Chapter 11 of the FTA establishes that each country will exempt the other from GATT Article XIX safeguard actions except in cases where the other is a substantial source of injury. However, in such case, imports may not be reduced below their trend "over a reasonable base period with allowance for growth."[9]

The two governments agree in Chapter 19 to "develop more effective rules and disciplines concerning the use of government subsidies" and to "develop a substitute system of rules dealing with unfair pricing . . ."[10] (i.e., dumping and predatory pricing) over five to seven years. In the interim, existing national laws will apply; however, judicial review of administrative agency findings will be replaced by binding review by binational panels.[11] Chapter 19 establishes these procedures, which are distinct from the general dispute settlement procedures established under Chapter 18.

Regarding foreign investment, the United States and Canada will afford each other's subsidiaries national treatment, except in some sensitive industries. Canada reserves the right to screen only *direct* acquisitions of its largest nonfinancial corporations and financial institutions. Trade-related performance requirements are prohibited (i.e., goals for import substitution, domestic sourcing or exports) but the issue of non-trade-related performance requirements remains unresolved.[12] Canada's cultural industries are exempt from the investment chapter and virtually all other provisions of the agreement.

In framing *new* practices and regulations affecting non-financial business services, the two countries will give each other's service providers national treatment and right of establishment and seek to ensure compatible licensing and certification requirements. The two governments will undertake negotiations to eliminate existing impediments to trade on a sector-by-sector basis.

Regarding financial services, U.S. firms will enjoy much greater freedom to expand in Canada.[13] As the two governments continue their processes of domestic deregulation and reregulation, they will seek to assure mutual benefits.

Focusing on other non-tariff barriers to trade in goods, the agreement provides a standstill on product standards inhibiting trade and the joint recognition of testing facilities. Bilaterally, it lowers the threshold for purchases covered by the GATT Procurement Code from $171,000 to $25,000; this does not affect the actions of the states and provinces. The FTA does not contain an intellectual property chapter.[14]

The United States and Canada will undertake bilateral negotiations to harmonize product standards for agricultural products and related commodities. For other goods, they will seek to make product standards more compatible and recognize each other's testing and certification bodies. The two governments agree to cooperate in the GATT to achieve progress on procurement and intellectual property and to expand the FTA provisions regarding procurement within one year of the conclusion of the Uruguay Round.

Chapter 18 establishes the Canada-United States Trade Commission. It is composed of the U.S. Trade Representative and the Canadian Minister for International Trade (or their designated representatives) and will mediate most disputes.[15] The first step will be consultations. Should these fail, either country may ask the Commission to take up the issue or seek resolution through the GATT. If the Commission fails to achieve a mutually satisfactory resolution within 30 days, a panel of five experts may be established to make recommendations; generally, their findings will be published. "Whenever possible, the resolution shall be non-implementation or removal of a measure not conforming with this Agreement ... or, failing such a resolution, compensation."[16] Binding arbitration is available if both parties agree. All disputed safeguard actions will be subject to binding arbitration.[17]

Labour Adjustments

Like other trade agreements, the FTA will improve economic efficiency by fostering greater specialization, but will impose labour adjustments. These are not expected to be large.

The adjustments imposed by the FTA may be divided into two general groups:

1. Interindustry adjustments that occur when whole industries expand and contract in response to new market opportunities and competition;

2. Intraindustry adjustments that occur as industries, firms and plants specialize in fewer products to serve broader North American markets and as more capable suppliers of specific products gain market shares.

Interindustry Adjustments

Two types of models have been used to estimate FTA interindustry labour adjustments—computable general equilibrium (CGE) models and macroeconomic models. Essentially, CGE models are superior to macro models for simulating shifts in employment opportunities among industries. However, they generally assume full employment and miss the positive effects of trade liberalization on aggregate employment and growth. These dynamic benefits, which are simulated by macro models, can offset some or all of the job losses in industries adversely affected by a redistribution of employment opportunities under the FTA.[18]

Among the most interesting estimates of interindustry labour adjustments are those obtained by Brown and Stern from a CGE model they constructed and those obtained by Magun and Rao of the Economic Council of Canada simulating its macroeconomic model.[19]

Brown and Stern's estimates of job losses in adversely affected industries are larger because their full employment assumption requires net gains/losses across industries to sum to zero.[20] In the Economic Council's model, a projected 1.8 per cent gain in economy-wide employment offsets many employment losses. Brown and Stern's results are a better indication which industries are likely to lose significant shares of employment; however, the absolute size of job losses will likely be much smaller than indicated. Indeed, Harris and Kwakwa's findings indicate that FTA labour adjustments could be significantly reduced or eliminated by moderate growth and normal employee turnover.[21]

Table 4 also presents results from industry studies undertaken for the 1985 Macdonald Royal Commission Report. These identified several Canadian industries as likely to experience employment gains—forest products, paper and urban mass transportation equipment—and employment losses—textiles, clothing and footwear, machinery and equipment, electronics and electrical machinery and equipment, furniture, scientific equipment and consumer products.[22] These are denoted by the letters "P" and "N" in the right-hand column of Table 4. Noticeably absent from the first group is the traditionally strong Canadian nonferrous metals industry.[23] At the time these studies were completed (April 1985), it already had fairly good access to the U.S. market and was already quite successful there; free trade was not seen by the authors as holding important new opportunities for Canadian producers.[24]

Table 4
The FTA's Estimated Long-Run Employment Effects

	Brown and Stern U.S.	Canada	Economic Council of Canada[1] (Canada only)	Industry Studies (Canada Only)[11]
	% change		% change	P=positive N=negative
Agriculture, Forestry and Fishing	-0.5	-5.6	1.44[2]	P
Mining & Quarrying	-0.5	-1.1	1.69	
Manufacturing	0.4	-0-.2	0.90	
Food, Beverages, Tobacco	0.0	-1.9	1.95[3]	
Textiles	3.9	-35.4	-2.19[4]	N
Clothing	0.7	-6.4	1.73	N
Leather Products	-0.6	4.9	-2.06	
Footwear	-0.5	2.2		N
Wood Products	0.5	-6.1	1.64	P
Furniture & Fixtures	0.8	-2.5	0.91	N
Paper Products	3.1	-19.3	0.61	P
Printing & Publishing	0.2	-3.3	6.08	
Chemicals	0.8	17.9	-0.34	
Petroleum Product	0.2	-11.6	0.77	
Rubber Products	0.1	-1.2	-1.72	
Nonmetallic Mineral Prods.	0.9	-16.8	1.55	
Glass Products	0.4	-3.9		
Iron & Steel	-0.5	28.5	2.93[5]	
Nonferrous Metals	-13.6	152.4		
Metal Products	0.7	-7.1	1.01	
Nonelectrical Machinery	-0.3	-1.2	0.66[6]	N
Electrical Machinery	1.2	-14.2	-3.38[7]	N
Transport Equipment	0.0	0.5	0.30	
Miscellaneous Manufactures	-0.5	7.3	-1.42	
Services	0.0	0.5	2.19	
Utilities	-0.3	0.1	1.34	
Construction	0.0	1.0	5.07	
Trade	-0.1	0.5	2.61[8]	
Transportation	0.0	0.5	1.77	
Financial Services	-0.1	0.4	1.86[9]	
Personal Services	0.0	0.5	0.95[10]	
Aggregate	0.0	0.0	1.80	

Notes

1. Industry classification taken from Brown and Stern. In manufacturing, except where noted, the Economic Council's classification system was quite similar. In primary and service sectors the Economic Council's classification system, as noted, was more desegregated.

2. Employment weighted average for agriculture (1.08), forestry (0.50) and fishing (0.88).

3. Food and beverages (2.00) and tobacco products (0.10).

4. Textiles (-2.05) and knitting mills (-2.64).

5. Primary metals.

6. Machinery.

7. Electrical products.

8. Retail trade (3.11), wholesale trade (2.34), accommodations (2.12), and amusement (1.71).

9. Business services (1.17) and other financial services (3.02).

10. Education and health (3.46) and other personal services (0.67).

11. For forest products a "P" was placed in the rows for forestry and wood products. For machinery and equipment an "N" was placed in the row for nonelectrical machinery. For electronics and electrical machinery and equipment an "N" was placed in the row for electrical machinery. Urban mass transportation equipment and scientific equipment only compose small segments of much larger industries and are not listed. Consumer products was too general to be classified.

Sources: Brown and Stern, "Computable General Equilibrium Estimates of the Gains from U.S.-Canadian Trade Liberalization"; Magun and Rao, "Assessment of the Economic Impact of the Canada-U.S. Free Trade Agreement."

Royal Commission on the Economic Union and Development Prospects for Canada, *Report.* Volume One. (Ottawa: Ministry of Supply and Services, 1985), pp. 336-49.

Focusing on the United States, Brown and Stern's results indicate the FTA will cause a modest increase in manufacturing employment at the expense of the primary sectors. Within manufacturing, their results indicate that only the nonferrous metals industry faces job losses greater than one per cent.

For Canada, both Brown and Stern's and the Economic Council's findings indicate that the FTA will accelerate the shift towards service activities; the impact on overall Canadian manufacturing employment should be minimal. Should the FTA have even a modest positive effect on long-run aggregate Canadian employment, the results of these two studies together indicate that the overall effect on Canadian manufacturing should be zero or positive.

Focusing on specific Canadian manufacturing industries, Brown and Stern's results indicate employment losses in five of the six industries represented both in their study and identified as vulnerable by the Macdonald Commission. The Economic Council's results indicate less than average (1.8 per cent) employment growth for each of these five industries.

Table 5
Simulated Impacts of the FTA on
Canadian Industries Designated as Vulnerable
by the Macdonald Commission

	Brown and Stern %	Economic Council of Canada %
Textiles	-35.4	-2.2
Clothing	-6.4	1.7
Footwear	2.2	
Furniture and Machinery	-2.5	0.9
Nonelectrical Machinery	-1.2	0.7
Electrical Machinery	-14.2	-3.4

In five other manufacturing industries, Brown and Stern's results indicate employment losses greater than 5 per cent—wood products (-6.1 per cent), paper (-19.3 per cent), petroleum products (-11.6 per cent), nonmetallic mineral products (-16.8 per cent) and fabricated metal products (-7.1 per cent). The Economic Council's findings indicate positive but below average employment growth in each of these sectors. Brown and Stern's pessimistic results for wood products, paper and petroleum products are surprising given Canada's traditionally strong export performance in these areas; whereas metal fabricated products and nonmetallic mineral products are industries in which Canadian imports substantially exceed exports.[25]

Summing up, it appears that the Canadian manufacturing industries most likely to face negative adjustments are *textiles, clothing, furniture and fixtures, electrical and nonelectrical equip-*

ment and machinery, nonmetallic mineral products, and *fabricated metal products.* However, the magnitude of actual job losses could be significantly circumscribed, and in some cases virtually eliminated, by moderate growth and the normal process of employee turnover.

Nevertheless, it should be recognized that other significant labour adjustment pressures, which were present before the FTA, will persist. As discussed in Chapter 4, these include the effects of changing comparative advantages and new manufacturing technologies which are significantly reducing labour requirements in many industrial activities. Also, short-term shifts in macro-economic conditions and exchange rates can have important destabilizing effects on manufacturing employment.

Intraindustry Adjustments

Although free trade will reduce the relative importance of many Canadian industries more than it will reduce their absolute employment, substantial adjustments will still occur within industries as firms and plants specialize in fewer items within product lines.

Focusing on efforts to lengthen production runs and increase economies of scale, it appears that many of these adjustments may be achieved through more specialized use of existing plants, as opposed to building new plants.[26] This implies fairly palatable adjustments for firms and workers.

Intraindustry adjustments will also result from the wide range of competitive capabilities among branches and even firms within Canadian industries. For example, the furniture industry, which the Macdonald Royal Commission designated as vulnerable, has two main branches—household and office. As the FTA came into force, the Canadian household branch was overdiversified and geared towards servicing the domestic market; a 12 per cent tariff helped limit imports to about one-fifth of the Canadian market, implying major adjustments under the FTA. Nevertheless, several firms were already oriented toward the upper end of the market, exporting most of what they made. These should profit from the elimination of tariffs.[27] Similarly, many Canadian office furniture manufacturers are highly competitive, exporting more than two-fifths of their output to the United States, and are likely to profit substantially from improved market access. Elsewhere, in the electronics and electrical machinery industries, Canadian-based producers of certain telecommunications apparatus and electricity-generating equipment are highly competitive and are expected to benefit from free trade.

Concluding Remarks

The FTA represents substantial progress toward a single U.S.-Canadian market for goods, services and capital. The elimination of tariffs, prohibitions on new import restrictions, export subsidies and embargoes, and a standstill on most other non-tariff measures should ensure that many of the benefits of duty-free trade are achieved. Guarantees of national treatment and right of establishment, as well as the joint commitment to avoid new discriminatory licensing, certification and regulatory procedures, should provide service firms with the necessary assurances about continued market access to undertake substantial new investments on both sides of the border. The provisions regarding foreign investment and financial services will bring the United States and Canada many of the benefits of fully integrated markets.

Canada achieved many of its goals in the free trade negotiations. It has substantially increased access to its most important market, and it has maintained latitude to promote cultural industries and screen acquisitions of its financial and largest nonfinancial companies. With regard to security of access, the global safeguard provisions reduce the likelihood that Canadian exports will be sideswiped by U.S. global actions. However, as discussed in Chapter 5, this provision may need tightening as it applies to U.S. efforts to negotiate voluntary restraint agreements.

The dispute settlement mechanism for subsidies and dumping should encourage impartial and moderate interpretations of both countries' laws and establish confidence in the objectivity of their application. Nevertheless, from Canada's perspective, several critical questions regarding subsidies do remain. In recent cases where Canadian exporters were found to benefit from subsidies, how often did political considerations actually tip the balance, not in the decision to bring suit, but in a finding that countervailable subsidies were present? How often did affirmative findings reflect an American view of countervailable subsidies, which is broader than the Canadian view yet consistent with U.S. law? How often did the product in question benefit from subsidies in both the United States and Canada?[28]

Studying U.S. countervailing duties from 1980 to 1986, Morici noted evidence of such problems in three of the five countervailing duties levied on Canadian products—softwood lumber, Atlantic groundfish and hogs.[29] More recently, the 1989 finding that Canadian pork products' producers benefit from a countervailable subsidy provides yet another example of such problems. Although crafting joint rules governing subsidies will be difficult and complex, these experiences indicate that the subsidies issue should remain high among Canadian priorities.

The United States can claim important progress, particularly with respect to provisions regarding foreign investment, financial services and product standards, and the comprehensive business services agreement. Prohibitions on export taxes, the dual pricing of exports and export embargoes will generally assure Americans access to Canadian energy at about the same prices as paid by Canadians under comparable commercial circumstances. Among the more notable shortcomings from a U.S. perspective is the absence of restrictions on foreign investment performance requirements having second order effects on trade (e.g., requirements relating to product mandates, R & D and technology transfers).

Although a great deal has been achieved, it is important to recognize that many of the benefits of the FTA are prospective. The agreement establishes an extensive agenda for cooperation and follow-on negotiations. The principal issues may be grouped as follows:

- The two governments are committed to developing substitute rules and disciplines for subsidies and dumping within five to seven years[30] and to reaching agreement to further liberalize government procurement within one year of the conclusion of the Uruguay Round.

- The two governments will seek to harmonize or make more compatible a broad range of policies and practices. These include efforts to achieve an open border for agricultural products, mutual recognition of product testing data, greater compatibility of product standards and technical regulations, further liberalization of business services, and cooperation in financial regulation.

- The two governments have agreed to cooperate in the GATT to achieve progress on agricultural subsidies, procurement and intellectual property.

- Finally, oversights and flaws in the agreement will become apparent over time. For example, the safeguards provisions may require tightening, or more formal institutional mechanisms may be required.[31]

Accepting the disciplines the FTA imposes, achieving further liberalization through negotiations and closing loopholes will not always be easy. Although the economic adjustments imposed by the FTA itself are not great, they come on top of other pressures acting on both economies. Global shifts in comparative advantages and accelerating technological change are reshaping the North American economy and posing perplexing new challenges for policy makers.

In Canada, detractors blame the FTA for the country's economic adjustment problems which, in fact, have much wider origins. This attitude in turn, is a contributing factor in dampening Canadian enthusiasm for free trade.

In the United States, mounting competitive pressures, increasing dependence on foreign technology and capital, and frustrations in negotiations with the EC and Japan are creating the political basis for nationalist policy responses. Should the United States turn in this direction, the character and impact of such responses are much broader than the focused tools of contingent protection that exemplified American protectionism in the 1970s and 1980s. As such, the re-emergence of economic nationalism in the United States would imply a much different and more complex set of challenges for Canadian policy makers.

A major turn in the United States toward *dirigiste* industrial policies would constitute the kind of policy development that historically has provoked a major reassessment of Canadian commercial policy.

In the 1990s, though, Canadians will have the context of the FTA process—consultations, dispute settlement and negotiations—to address the American challenge. As discussed in Chapter 6, the processes described here re-establish the special relationship and do so in ways that are consistent with contemporary global and bilateral challenges. It is to these we now turn.

Notes

1. Canada, Minister for External Affairs, *Canadian Trade Negotiations,* (Ottawa: Department of External Affairs, 1985), pp. 3-4 and 25-27.

2. In 1988, then Treasury Secretary James Baker stated: "This agreement is also a lever to achieve more open trade. Other nations are forced to recognize that the United States will devise ways to expand trade—with or without them. If they choose not to open markets, they will not reap the benefits." *The International Economy,* Vol. II, No. 1 (January/February 1988), p. 41.

3. In 1987, at the conclusion of the Tokyo Round tariff cuts, average Canadian tariffs on U.S. imports were 9 to 10 per cent; the comparable figures for the United States were 4 to 5 per cent. Ambassador Clayton Yeutter, *Testimony Before the Senate Committee on U.S.-Canada Trade Negotiations* (April 11, 1986), p. 3.

4. The United States also sought to end: discrimination against the marketing of U.S. liquor, wine and beer; barriers to U.S. exports of poultry, eggs, dairy products and red meats; and seasonal tariffs on fresh fruits and vegetables. The FTA addresses U.S. concerns about liquor, wine, red meats, fresh fruits and vegetables but not beer, poultry, eggs and dairy products.

   The United States also looked for resolution of a number of other bilateral issues, including better protection for U.S. pharmaceutical patents and copyright protection for U.S. broadcasters whose signals are retransmitted in Canada.

5. The section is not intended to be a complete summary of the FTA. Readers requiring one can refer to Peter Morici, "The Canada-U.S. Free Trade Agreement," *The International Trade Journal,* Vol. III, No. 4 (Summer 1989).

6. Rules of origin require materials and components imported from third countries to be incorporated into other goods or transformed in physically or commercially significant ways. In most cases, this is achieved if a production process results in a change in tariff classification, or as a backup requirement, if it results in a 50 per cent U.S./Canadian value-added. However, the tougher 50 per cent rule is required for automotive products, and the FTA limits the amount of apparel made from offshore fabric that qualifies for duty-free treatment.

7. In the event of shortages, supplies must be shared on the basis of consumption patterns for the previous three years. Also, subject to GATT disciplines, both countries may restrict exports of logs, and Quebec and the Atlantic provinces may restrict exports of unprocessed fish.

8. Under the *Automotive Agreement of 1965*, Canada essentially affords duty-free treatment to all the imports of firms that assemble one car in Canada for each car sold there and achieve value-added in Canada equal to 60 per cent of their sales in Canada. The United States affords duty-free treatment to the Canadian made products of firms meeting a 50 per cent U.S./Canadian value-added requirement. The incentives for Chrysler, General Motors and Ford to meet the Canadian safeguards are: (1) duty-free access for U.S. produced cars; and (2) duty-free access for off-shore imports. Among the major foreign makers of passenger vehicles, only Volvo qualifies for these benefits.

    By meeting the old Canadian content rules, the three major North American companies and Volvo may continue to bring captive imports into Canada duty free. In the FTA, Canada agrees not to extend such benefits to other foreign passenger vehicle manufacturers.

9. FTA Article 1102, paragraph 4.b.

10. FTA Article 1907, paragraph 1.

11. Changes in laws will apply to Canada (the United States) only if Canada (the United States) is specifically named and such changes are consistent with the GATT and the general intent of the FTA.

    Binational panels will examine agency findings to ensure that they are "in accordance with the antidumping or countervailing duty law of the importing country." FTA Article 1904, paragraph 2.

    For detailed analyses of this review process see the papers by Debra P. Steger, Shirley A. Coffield, Richard G. Dearden, and Gary Horlick and Debra A. Valentine in Donald M. McRae and Debra P. Steger (eds.), *Understanding the Free Trade Agreement* (Ottawa: The Institute for Research on Public Policy, 1988).

12. Canadian officials maintain that other performance requirements such as undertakings concerning product mandates, R & D spending, and technology transfer are now accepted and legitimized because the FTA does not prohibit them. U.S. officials do not share this view.

13. Most remaining barriers to north-south financial integration that remain now emanate from domestic regulations posing impediments to efficient domestic markets—e.g., U.S. constraints on interstate banking and the Glass-Steagall Act which separates investment and commercial banking in the United States.

14. The FTA does provide for better protection for U.S. pharmaceutical patents and copyright protection for U.S. broadcast signals in Canada.

15. Disputes concerning subsidy/countervailing duties and antidumping duties are subject to a separate binding dispute settlement mechanism. Disputes relating to financial services will be resolved through consultations between the Departments of Finance and Treasury. The decisions of Investment Canada with respect to acquisitions are final and may not be appealed through the FTA dispute settlement procedure.

16. FTA Article 1807, paragraph 8.

17. For detailed explanations of this dispute settlement procedure the reader is referred to the papers by L.H. Legault, Robert E. Hudec and Julius Katz in McRae and Steger (eds.), *Understanding the Free Trade Agreement.*

18. These issues are discussed in Morici, "The Canada-U.S. Trade Agreement," pp. 347-373.

19. Drusilla K. Brown and Robert M. Stern, "Computable General Equilibrium Estimates of the Gains from U.S.-Canadian Trade Liberalization," presented at Lehigh University Conference on Economic Aspects of Regional Trading Arrangements, Bethlehem, Penn, May 25-27, 1988; Sunder Magun and Someshwar Rao, "Assessment of the Economic Impact of the Canada-U.S. Free Trade Agreement," presented at the North American Economics and Finance Association Meeting, New York, December 28-31, 1988. The Economic Council study, like most others, does not provide sectoral estimates for the United States.

20. Employment rises in those industries with increases in new exports and domestic sales; it falls in industries losing domestic market shares to imports.

21. See Richard G. Harris and Victoria Kwakwa, "The 1988 Canada-United States Free Trade Agreement: A Dynamic General Equilibrium Evaluation of the Transition Effects," presented at the NBER/CERP Conference on Strategic Trade Policy, (Cambridge, Mass.: National Bureau of Economic Research, July 8-9, 1988).

22. Royal Commission on the Economic Union and Developments Prospects for Canada, *Report*, Vol. One, pp. 336-49.

23. Also omitted are energy products and ferrous metals. During the early 1980s, energy trade was considered to be restrained primarily by Canada's National Energy Program and regulatory activities that were thought to lie outside the likely agenda for free trade discussions. In steel, U.S. non-tariff barriers are important. The United States has taken safeguard actions in specialty steel, and a "gentleman's agreement" has evolved imposing flexible limits on Canada's basic steel exports. Also significant in the resource area, a

15 per cent excise tax has been imposed on Canadian softwood lumber exports to pre-empt U.S. countervailing duties. The FTA has not had immediate impacts on these measures.

24. See Gilbert R. Winham, *Canada-U.S. Sectoral Trade Study: The Impact of Free Trade* (Halifax: Centre for Foreign Policy Studies, Dalhousie University, 1986), pp. 81-82.

25. Canada, Department of Finance, *The Canada-U.S. Free Trade Agreement: An Economic Assessment* (Ottawa, 1988), p. 9.

26. In 1979, Daly concluded that the absence of adequate product-specific economies of scale was a much more important cause of the U.S.-Canadian manufacturing productivity gap than an absence of optimum size plants or firm-specific economies of scale in Canada. Similarly, other studies indicate that in 1979 only about 20 per cent of Canadian manufacturing took place in suboptimal size plants, imposing an overall cost disadvantage of about 4 per cent; Magun and Rao maintain that these figures fell during the 1980s. Studying industrial adaptation to the Kennedy Round tariff cuts in the 1970s, Baldwin and Gorecki found that firms facing increased import competition tended to reduce product diversity and lengthen production runs rather than increase plant size.

      See Donald J. Daly, *Canada's Comparative Advantage*. Discussion Paper No. 135 (Ottawa: Economic Council of Canada, September 1979), p. 28; Magun and Rao, "Assessment of the Economic Impact of the Canada-U.S. Free Trade Agreement," pp. 44-47 and 56-58; John R. Baldwin and Paul Gorecki, "The Relationship Between Trade and Tariff Patterns and the Efficiency of the Canadian Manufacturing Sector in the 1970s: A Summary," in John Whalley (ed.), *Canada-United States Trade* (Toronto: University of Toronto Press for the Royal Commission on the Economic Union and Development Prospects for Canada, 1985), p. 187; and Morici, *The Global Competitive Struggle*, p. 81.

27. Royal Commission on the Economic Union and Development Prospects for Canada, *Report*, p. 345.

28. When a product benefits from subsidies in both countries and imports from Canada are found to injure U.S. producers, the U.S. countervailing duty is levied on the full value of the Canadian subsidy and not the difference between the two national subsidies.

29. The five products countervailed were softwood lumber, fresh Atlantic groundfish, hogs, gas and oil well tubular steel products, and carnations. Softwood lumber involved a resource pricing problem, an area where the two governments have developed different views about what should constitute a countervailable subsidy. Also, the finding of a subsidy with regard to stumpage pricing, just four years after a similar complaint had failed, ignited latent Canadian concerns about the politicization of the administration of U.S. trade laws. Two other cases, fresh Atlantic groundfish and hogs, provide important examples where industries

in both countries benefit from government subsidies. See Morici, "U.S.-Canadian Trade Relations in the 1980s," pp. 159-180.

30. Since the agreement went into force in January 1989, the effective deadline is January 1996.

31. As currently structured, the Canada-United States Trade Commission is supported by two separate secretariats (one in the Department of Commerce and another in External Affairs), and only on matters pertaining to Article 18 and 19 dispute settlement. There is no provision for joint record-keeping, archiving Commission decisions and panel reports, or joint study and technical analysis of disputes before the Commission.

Chapter 4

Coping with the Global Economy

The United States and Canada are creating a single market at a time of fundamental change in the global economy. Economic, political and technological developments are combining to alter radically the environment confronting North American industries. These trends are significantly changing assessments of national interests and the best ways to serve them.

The Canada-U.S. Free Trade Agreement is a regional agreement but not a regionally motivated one. U.S. and Canadian decisions to enter into the FTA emanated from distinctive national views of the challenges posed by global competition and stress in the General Agreement on Tariffs and Trade system, and by Canadian perceptions of the U.S. responses to these challenges. In many ways, the success of the FTA will hinge on how effectively the two national governments can use the agreement to manage their commercial relationship in the context of global competition and their broader multilateral policy goals.

Effective management has many dimensions. It certainly encompasses mediating disputes amicably and forging joint rules that establish consistent expectations on the part of policy makers and businesses. However, as global economic pressures and bilateral competition for investment and jobs mount, effective management may also require a greater element of cooperation in

83

coping with adjustments and building viable industries than heretofore considered necessary or desirable. As adjustment pressures on communities increase and are translated into political pressures on national, state and provincial leaders to act, cooperative approaches may prove to be the most effective way to address economic distress and new opportunities while avoiding national policy responses that are competitive and predatory in a binational context.

This will not be easy. In the 1990s, U.S. and Canadian policies may be out of sync. Washington may be forced to play a greater role in financing industrial R & D and assisting high-technology activities generally. Ottawa, facing even greater fiscal exigencies than Washington and preoccupied with defining a new relationship with Quebec, will likely continue the path established in the 1980s of moderate industrial policies. However, devolution of economic authority to Quebec or all the provinces could lead to greater diversity in Canadian responses. Nevertheless, the likelihood that Washington will lead North American intervention is raised by:

- Mounting pressures within the Congress and the U.S. business community for federal action.

- The decided emphasis on supporting the development of precompetitive technologies—as opposed to band-aids for rust bowl activities—in Japanese and European industrial strategies.[1]

- The high costs and institutional barriers many U.S. firms seem to encounter in undertaking precompetitive research and product development.

The FTA establishes the context for achieving U.S.-Canadian cooperation. In follow-on negotiations, the two national governments can establish ways to mediate differences in approaches to industrial and regional adjustment and to foster cooperation in R & D. In the United States, the FTA, by re-establishing the special relationship, provides the basis for offering Canadian firms the opportunity to participate in programs ordinarily closed to other foreign companies. For example, in legislation proposed in 1990 to permit antitrust exemption for joint production by large U.S. multinational corporations (MNCs), Canadian firms, unlike other foreign firms, would be permitted to participate. The Microelectronics & Computer Technology Corporation, a research consortium of 21 firms, has opened to Canadian participation. In both cases, the FTA was the motivating factor.

This chapter examines the place of the United States and Canada in the global economy. The first two parts survey changing U.S. and Canadian comparative advantage and key developments in the international trading system. This is followed by analyses of the impacts of accelerating change and globalization on competition among firms and American industrial policy responses of particular importance to Canada. Chapter 5 explores the consequences of these developments for bilateral relations and the ways the FTA might evolve to address this new environment.

Changing Comparative Advantages
The United States

During the 1970s, imports captured growing shares of U.S. markets for the products of mature industries such as apparel, footwear, steel, and compact cars. An expectation emerged among economists and policy makers that the United States could pay for these imports and higher priced foreign oil by relying on exports of agricultural products, high technology goods, and services. Shifts in comparative advantages and government policies at home and abroad have frustrated these expectations.

Briefly, improved agricultural productivity in many middle income developing countries, coupled with the effects of farm support programs in the United States, Canada, the European Community, and Japan, reduced agriculture's share of U.S. exports from 24 per cent in 1973-74 to 19 per cent in 1981 and 11 per cent in 1989.

High-technology products have become an increasingly important component of U.S. exports—rising from 16 per cent in 1973 to about 35 per cent in the late 1980s. However, imports of these products have grown even more rapidly, as Japan and many western European countries have expanded their R & D infrastructures at a faster rate than the United States.

U.S. industries such as microelectronics, telecommunications, aerospace, and computers have been the targets of government efforts in Japan and the EC to improve competitiveness.

Although these practices are not the principal cause of declining U.S. dominance in high-technology products, they have been the focus of considerable scrutiny by business leaders, trade negotiators and the Congress as U.S. competitive advantages have narrowed. Moreover, the success of some Japanese and European efforts are winning converts within the U.S. corporate community and leaders in Congress.

Specifically, the cost of undertaking precompetitive research in basic technologies, which generally have payoffs in widely diverse industrial applications, has been skyrocketing. For example, basic semiconductor projects can generate product development opportunities in industries as diverse as personal computers, video cassette recorders, household appliances, cameras, and avionics. When undertaken by one or a few companies in the same industry, precompetitive research has clear, non-appropriable benefits—specifically, precompetitive research creates generic technologies and profit-making opportunities in industries unrelated to the businesses financing the research. Frontier projects that could be undertaken for two or three million dollars in the early 1970s can cost more that 100 times that amount in the early 1990s. Non-appropriability, high costs and long gestation periods put many projects beyond the reach of individual companies that once funded major U.S. research initiatives such as Bell and General Electric.

Japanese and EC industrial policies have placed considerable emphasis on overcoming the barriers to private sector financing by bringing together groups of companies to undertake precompetitive research in areas such as semiconductors, computers, biotechnology, and new materials. Moreover, in Japan the vertical and horizontal scope of Japanese industrial groups—the *keiretsus*—ensures that more of the benefits of research accrue to the companies that bear the cost of projects. U.S. government efforts have been less oriented toward fostering business cooperation and more focused on ensuring defence, as opposed to commercial, capabilities. Similarly, the more specialized structure of U.S. industrial organizations provides fewer opportunities for spreading the costs, risks and benefits of precompetitive research.

Precompetitive research has always created broad externalities: breakthroughs in the Bell laboratories in the 1950s helped create the modern computer industry. In the 1950s and 1960s, though, private American laboratories were in a better position to undertake precompetitive research that created broad non-appropriable benefits because it was cheaper and foreign competitors were not as well supported or organized to gain greater proprietary benefits from such research. Also, when U.S. companies dominated world markets, they were better able to pass along the cost of research that benefited other industries in the form of higher prices to consumers. In the case of AT&T, it was able to tax consumers through regulated phone rates. In the 1980s and 1990s, it would seem that Japanese industrial policy and industrial structure better position Japanese firms to undertake precompetitive research.

At the next stage in the R & D process, the costs of developing new products and implementing new processes are skyrocketing. As discussed later in this chapter, U.S., Canadian and foreign firms are displaying a new agility in establishing cooperative efforts and alliances with rivals at home and abroad to stretch research budgets. Many are demonstrating that they can co-operate effectively with rivals.

Together, these trends have fed interest among American companies in a more aggressive federal policy for precompetitive research like the Sematech project in semiconductors. As discussed below, the Reagan Administration took some steps to increase the federal role in fostering commercial technology and industrial cooperation but the Bush Administration has displayed insensitivity to the private sector's aspirations for initiatives. The United States lags behind Japan and Germany in the spending on R & D overall and commercial R & D in particular; this gap is growing with important implications for the evolution of U.S. comparative advantages.

Business service exports—e.g., fees and royalties, financial and professional services, and travel and transportation—have not grown dramatically.[2] Government practices lying outside GATT jurisdiction have limited many foreign sales. Although the trade in services will likely be the focus of broad agreements in the Uruguay Round, the processes of actually reducing impediments to trade in many areas will require difficult harmonization of domestic policies and progress will likely be slow.

With regard to the future of U.S. comparative advantages in services, the creation of new products that exploit rapidly changing information/communications technologies have helped U.S. industries maintain leads. But other factors are also important to competitiveness—notably, a well educated, technologically experienced, internationally aware labour force.

The declining performance of U.S. elementary and secondary schools is a critical liability. For example, in math, science and world geography, American students generally score below students from other industrialized countries on international tests. The poor performance of public schools has been declared a threatening competitive liability by the U.S. government.[3] As the educational attainments of workers in Japan and newly industrializing countries (NICs) continue to rise and their experience with technology-intensive manufacturing grow, the United States will encounter even more intense competition.[4] Japanese and some European banks' superior access to capital places U.S. banks at a competitive disadvantage.

The U.S. economy will be more balanced in the 1990s than was anticipated in the 1970s and early 1980s. Weakened competitive advantages in agriculture and knowledge-intensive activities imply improved competitive performance in other industries. Employment and value-added in mature, import-competing industries, such as automotive products and textiles, will be higher than would have been the case in the absence of these shifts in comparative advantages.

Nevertheless, adjustment pressures will persist. New computer-based manufacturing technologies are greatly reducing labour requirements. Exacerbating the effects of these trends, the advent of substitutes for many basic metal, paper, ceramic, and glass products are reducing the demand for the products of these industries. Even in manufacturing industries with expanding sales, we may expect to see only modest employment gains and in some cases overall employment will decline. These problems will be particularly acute when monetary polices encourage a stronger dollar than is consistent with longer-term trends in U.S. competitiveness.

Owing to substantial variations among companies in their abilities to harness effectively new technologies and business formats, not all firms and workers will fare equally well within particular industries. Often, offshore investors will be in a better position to exploit market opportunities than North American companies—consider, for example, Honda and General Motors in the automobile industry. The reallocation of employment opportunities among the communities with strong employers and those with weak ones will exacerbate dislocations in the job market.

In a bilateral context, economic adjustments that push U.S. industrial activity towards greater emphasis on mature manufacturing place U.S. and Canadian firms, workers and communities in direct competition. These factors magnify the potential consequences of business incentives offered in both countries to attract plants and jobs and increase the importance of achieving a bilateral understanding with regard to locational subsidies, countervailing duties and other development policy tools.

Particularly significant are prospects for the nonferrous metals and steel industries. New materials and advances in microelectronics have substantially reduced the demand for copper, lead, zinc, and other nonferrous metals, and steel. Minimills provide an important substitute for the products of large integrated mills by recycling the steel imported through motor vehicles. The downsizing of cars has had the same general consequences for steel and some nonferrous metals.[5] The decline in the exchange rate for the dollar from 1985 to 1988 and the length of the economic expansion helped improve sales of domestic producers. The longer-term prospects for growth in North American consumption of most nonferrous metals and steel remain severely limited.

Canada

Historically, Canada's competitive strengths have emanated from its resource endowments—farm and fish products, forest products, minerals, and metals. However, prospects for these exports are limited.

In agriculture, Canadian grain producers are more dependent on foreign markets than American farmers, yet they too must cope with slow-growing export markets. Prospects for substantial expansion of forest products exports appear constrained by timber supplies. The advent of substitute materials and new technologies are limiting market growth for important Canadian metal exports—e.g., nickel, copper, zinc, and lead—and increased competitive capacity in developing countries has reduced Canadian market shares for most of these products. Environmental concerns have considerably reduced the prospects for the important asbestos industry and will require major new investments in industries such as pulp and paper. During the 1980s, export prices for most of these products were flat or falling. The contribution of natural resources to Canadian exports has fallen from 65 per cent in 1960, to 47 per cent in 1970 and just 35 per cent in 1987.[6]

Focusing on secondary manufactures, automotive sales have fluctuated significantly but have averaged about one quarter of Canadian exports over the past two decades. Meanwhile, other manufactures' share increased from 10 per cent in 1960 to 16 per cent in 1970 to over 20 per cent in recent years. This reflects improved Canadian comparative advantages in secondary manufacturing.

In continuing this industrial transformation, Canadian manufacturers face many of the same challenges as their U.S. counterparts but they are in a weaker position. In 1988, Canadian manufacturing productivity stood at about 70 per cent of U.S. levels, about the same level as in 1970. Underspecialization and slow dissemination of new technology have historically been key problems. To improve performance, Canadian firms must accelerate rationalization and the implementation of new methods such as computer-assisted systems.[7]

As in the United States, labour adjustment pressures will persist as new technologies reduce labour requirements even in expanding industries and new competitors with better mastery of product design and process technology capture market shares from established employers. Also, being so much more vulnerable to foreign competition, exchange rate fluctuations which are driven by short-term macroeconomic policies—as opposed to longer-term fundamentals, such as relative rates of wage inflation and productivity growth—can play an even more destabilizing role in Canadian manufacturing employment than in the United States. For example, in the late 1980s, the Bank of Canada's firm anti-inflation policy pushed up the value of the Canadian currency against the U.S. dollar, the yen and European currencies placing Canadian manufacturing at a decided cost disadvantage.[8] Canadian manufacturing employment, after climbing from 1.66 to 2.00 million from March 1983 to June 1989, fell to 1.57 million in

March 1991. By way of comparison, manufacturing employment, during the last downturn, dropped from 1.92 to 1.62 million between June 1981 and January 1983.9

The FTA is encouraging long-term structural improvements in Canadian manufacturing; however, it is adding to secular and cyclical adjustment pressures. As discussed in Chapter 3, short-term exchange rate fluctuations notwithstanding, econometric studies indicate that tariff cuts will accentuate the shift in Canadian employment away from resource industries towards service activities, leaving manufacturing's overall share of employment virtually unchanged from what it would have been without the FTA. Within manufacturing, the FTA could induce important interindustry adjustments. For example, textiles, apparel, furniture, and electrical and nonelectrical machinery and equipment face losses in employment shares.

The International Trading System

As U.S. and Canadian competitive advantages have diminished in areas of traditional export strength, Washington and Ottawa have sought improved foreign market access through the GATT.

The GATT and the Uruguay Round

The United States worked hard to put agricultural support reform, government procurement, intellectual property rights, industrial subsidies, product standards, and services on the Uruguay Round agenda. Canada, seeking to take better advantage of remaining strengths in resource-based products and a variety of specialized manufacturing and service activities, has been a valuable ally and has played a strong independent role. Although some kind of agreement or undertaking could still be achieved for many of the above mentioned issues, substantial progress will likely be slow for several reasons.

First, since the 1950s, the number and range of development characteristics of the GATT membership has grown significantly. Along with slower growth over the last two decades in North America and Europe, this magnifies the adjustment costs additional trade liberalization would impose. Changes in the composition of GATT membership also fuels political resistance to liberalization in North American and European communities long dependent on the steel, nonferrous metals, automobiles, consumer products, and other trade-impacted industries.

Second, many newly industrializing and developing countries bring different priorities to the negotiating table than developed countries. Among the countries within each of these groups there are significant differing points of view. Such differences strongly affect the importance governments attach to, or even their desire to see, progress on agricultural support policies, industrial subsidies, services, the protection of intellectual property, and safeguards and grey-area trade measures.

Third, progress on many non-tariff measures, such as standards and intellectual property, will often require harmonization or at least greater compatibility among national policies, practices and regulations. This creates difficulties because national practices frequently vary in their approach and rigor, even when goals are similar. More importantly, though, national governments sometimes differ on the basic goals for public policies.[10]

Fourth, the European Community 1992 initiative is taxing the Community's political and administrative resources and its capacity for adjustment, is reducing, at least in the short run, its ability to aggressively support multilateral liberalization.

Fifth, systemic codification of market disciplines has been a persistent U.S. goal in the GATT. Although the American notion that national policies should be responsive to market signals has gained currency in recent years, major U.S. trading partners frequently do not share U.S. views about what constitutes market-responsive policies.[11]

Consequently, the United States faces tough challenges in exerting needed leadership on issues where:

- U.S. perceptions differ substantially from European, East Asian and/or developing countries (e.g., subsidies and intellectual property);

- where the United States is perceived to have more to gain (e.g., services and agriculture);

- where the harmonization of domestic practices with strong cultural underpinnings is critical (e.g., product standards, regulation of public services and access to domestic distribution systems).

Certainly, these factors do not make multilateral progress impossible. However, they do make further meaningful liberalization difficult and the extension of regional agreements such as the FTA and the EC 1992 program attractive to policy makers.[12] Three major integrated regional markets are emerging—the expanded EC, the United States/Canada (perhaps with the addition of Mexico and other Latin American economies) and an informal East and Southeast Asian trading area (discussed below).

EC 1992 and the Opening of Eastern Europe

As a consequence of EC 1992, European firms will pose a much greater challenge to North American based production. Companies such as Ford, General Electric and Northern Telecom already approach Europe as one market, whereas many EC-based competitors, enjoying safe and protected national markets, often had more parochial strategies. Through a flurry of mergers and cross-border alliances, these firms are now taking aim at the entire European market,[13] and will be more able competitors outside the EC as well.

The opening up of Eastern Europe offers Western European firms access to an inexpensive, yet skilled labour force. The combination of Western European capital and technology and Eastern European labour provides production opportunities not currently available within the Canada-U.S. free-trade area. The population of Eastern Europe (less the Soviet Union) is about 135 million—accelerated industrial development there could portend adjustment pressures for industrialized countries as large as those created by the East Asian NICs in the 1980s.

Moreover, the 1992 process alone will give European firms better access to the 330 million person EC market than Canadian firms will have to the U.S. market of 240 million people under the FTA. Regarding non-tariff measures, Canadian firms may find themselves at the same kind of market access disadvantage as they did with respect to tariffs when the EC and European Free Trade Association were formed in the 1960s. This provides strong incentives for Canadian firms to globalize operations by investing heavily in the United States and the EC to assure market access. It could motivate Canadian policy makers to seek even greater harmonization of domestic policies and regulations with the United States than currently envisioned under the FTA, raising a variety of delicate sovereignty issues for Canadian political leaders.

Mexico and Latin America

In the late 1980s, Mexico began a process of internal economic reforms, reducing subsidies and restrictions on foreign investment, slashing tariffs and eliminating import quotas. Political stability in Mexico is critically dependent on the success of these economic reforms, and in turn their success is critically dependent on expanding manufactured exports to the United States. U.S. national interests are clear—political stability in Mexico is vital to U.S. security. Therefore, the Bush Administration's warm reception to Mexico's request for discussions to examine a free trade area was not surprising.

Political considerations aside, Mexico offers the United States some of the same kinds of opportunities that Eastern Europe offers the EC—a large and growing market of 85 million and inexpensive labour. As discussed in Chapter 5, a Mexico-U.S. free trade agreement could erode some of the benefits Canada anticipates under the FTA and provides Canada with strong motivations to join in these negotiations.

Elsewhere in Latin America, Chile, Brazil and other countries are liberalizing their import policies, and Caribbean and Central American countries have expressed interest in increasing access to the U.S. market. For its part, the Bush Administration sees trade liberalization and regional agreements as one important vehicle for fostering development in Latin America.

Other Developments

Trade and investment ties are growing among Japan and the emerging industrial centres of East and Southeast Asia. Despite the importance of the North American market to the industrial progress of Asia, intraregional trade accounted for 35 per cent of the region's export growth from 1965 to 1988, whereas North American trade accounted for only 29 per cent.[14] Japan, now the world's largest source of foreign aid, places 65 per cent of its aid in Asia.[15] These trends, along with growing ties between Japanese MNCs and Asian centres of industrialization, are creating a third major regional trading area. These developments are likely making some markets even more difficult for North American producers to penetrate.

The emergence of trading blocs centred in Europe by the EC and in Asia by Japan will increase pressure on the United States to liberalize trade first with Mexico and then perhaps with other Latin American countries.

For Canada, slow progress in the GATT and the consolidation of regional arrangements abroad further heighten the importance of access to the U.S. market and achieving substantial progress in follow-on FTA negotiations regarding subsidies, dumping, procurement, standards, and other non-tariff issues. As discussed in Chapters 5 and 6, Canada may identify advantages in joining the United States in regional initiatives to protect its stake in the U.S. market.

Technology and Competition

Along with regionalization, rapidly evolving communication/information technologies, computer-assisted manufacturing and the soaring costs of developing new products are combining to give increased impetus to mergers, corporate alliances and the globalization of enterprises. The combined effects of these developments make the industrial adjustments to changing competitive opportunities more subtle, far-reaching and perplexing than the mere expansion of some industrial activities and the contraction of others. For Canada, as always, the policy responses of the United States are critical in defining its policy challenges and options.

The Impact of New Technologies

Computer-based technologies, such as information management and computer-numerical control systems, have opened broad new opportunities in service and manufacturing industries alike.

In services, North American firms, often less bound by tradition than competitors abroad, have led in new product development and marketing. Consider, for example, the much more efficient retail and wholesale distribution systems in the United States and Canada. North American telecommunications companies like Teleglobe and Pacific Telesis set their sights far beyond this continent.[16] Despite the problems posed by developing country debt and the superior access to capital enjoyed by Japanese institutions, deregulation has cultivated an innovative and agile U.S. financial sector—U.S. investment and commercial bankers have led in the introduction of new products and funds transfer services.[17] In Canada, deregulation of the securities and investment banking industries should permit Canadian firms to participate in this progress; Canada's commercial banks remain able competitors.

Turning to manufacturing, the benefits of computer-assisted technologies appear to be less widely dispersed in the United States and Canada than in Japan and several northern European countries. North American firms appear, on average, to be achieving fewer improvements in flexibility, productivity and quality.[18]

In Japan, computer-assisted technologies have generally been introduced incrementally as individual devices could justify their cost. The transition from traditional manufacturing formats, though widespread, has been gradual within plants. North American manufacturers, under pressure to catch up, have often implemented new technologies in larger doses (the so-called "the moon shot approach"), converting or building whole lines at once. This often results in less flexibility and fewer productivity gains.[19] Nevertheless, there are good North American models such as Motorola[20] and Westinghouse.[21] North American firms vary considerably in their abilities to effectively use new manufacturing technologies.

Small manufacturers are encountering the greatest difficulties. For example, an Economic Council of Canada study of automation from 1980 to 1985 found that the likelihood of use of computer-based technology increased with company size.[22] In a study of computerized automation in 1368 U.S. machinery manufacturing plants, Kelley and Brooks found the typical firm failing to adopt this technology to be a small, single plant firm. The high cost of installing and mastering new systems appears prohibitive for many small firms.[23]

These findings underline two important realities. First, they highlight the difficulties of playing catch-up ball once foreign or domestic competitors have a head start with new technologies. This is an important reason why we may expect to see continued significant variations among North American firms in their abilities to keep pace with offshore competitors. Second, computer-assisted automation frees manufacturers from the need to sell large volumes of a few standardized items to achieve economies of scale. However, such automation still requires large volumes, even if spread across many product variants, to cover the costs of machinery and amassing the technical expertise and practical experience necessary to master these radical new approaches to manufacturing.[24]

Getting down to the level of basic industrial policy, new manufacturing technologies do not free most small- and medium-sized Canadian manufacturers, oriented primarily toward the domestic market, from the need to achieve greater economies of scale through exports. Unimpeded access to large foreign markets remains critical. Catching up with American and offshore competitors will be difficult for many Canadian manufacturers, and considerable intraindustry adjustments will result as more able Canadian firms and foreign subsidiaries expand their market shares at the expense of others.

Mergers and International Alliances

The costs of developing new products are soaring. For example, in the 1970s, a new drug typically cost $16 million and took four to five years to develop—today, the price tag is $250 million with a 12 year development period.[25] Only very large companies with well developed global marketing and production capabilities can support this scale of risk. Such considerations have driven a wave of mergers, alliances and joint ventures. For example, in pharmaceuticals these include Bristol-Myers Squibb, SmithKline Beckman,[26] and Merieux Connaught.

In addition, large and small companies alike are seeking joint venture partners to stretch research budgets, acquire product designs, achieve market access, and gain access to advanced manufacturing know-how. What is critical here is that, much more frequently than in the past, these joint ventures involve the participants' "core" products, technologies and markets, as arch rivals in one setting become partners in another. Focusing on the Canadian experience, Geringer and Woodcock conclude:

> Traditionally, many joint ventures were formed to exploit peripheral markets or technologies, their activities being of marginal importance to the maintenance of a parent firm's comparative advantage. A large portion of the joint ventures formed in the 1980s, however, involve primary or "core" activities of the parent firms, and they often link firms that are potential competitors.[27]

In a significant example, Texas Instruments, after suing Hitachi for patent infringement in 1986, is teaming up with its former nemesis to develop a 16 megabit RAM chip.[28] Semiconductor manufacturers already spend about 35 per cent of their research budget through similar technical alliances.[29]

Regarding market access, Northern Telecom has established a beachhead in the EC market through its $1 billion stake in STC PLC.[30] The Canadair Aerospace group is studying the feasibility of producing the CL-215T amphibian water bomber in a joint venture with Indonesia's state-owned aircraft maker to help assure access to the Southeast Asian market.[31]

Turning to advanced manufacturing technologies, usually there is no good substitute for experience. This an important reason why, despite Herculean efforts, GM cars averaged 1.4 more defects than Japanese cars in 1988.[32] Gaining access to Japanese manufacturing expertise was an important motivation for GM in undertaking a joint venture with Toyota in Fremont, California. In another joint venture initiated in 1986, Motorola gave Toshiba access to its prized microprocessor designs in exchange for Toshiba's dynamic random-access memory chips (DRAMs) manufacturing technology and better access to the Japanese market.[33] Reflecting the breadth of this trend, IBM has joined with Toshiba in its *first* joint production venture ever.[34]

What Makes a Competitive Firm?

For even the largest MNCs, the high costs of developing new products and assimilating new processes make national markets too limited. Large MNCs are increasingly involved in cooperative relationships with competitors, customers and suppliers, because not even the largest companies have the resources to cover all the bases. Arch rivals in one market become partners in another. Small companies increasingly rely on larger customers for capital, expertise and stable markets for their products.

U.S and Canadian firms vary substantially in their abilities to manage global operations, develop new technologies, assimilate new production and marketing methods, and participate in collaborative research and production arrangements of various kinds.[35] In mature industries and technology-intensive industries alike, some North American companies show great promise to be every bit as competitive as their foreign counterparts—e.g., Northern Telecom, Westinghouse, General Electric, and Ford. Even within companies, there is considerable variation in performance among divisions and plants. For example, a key part of GE's corporate strategy is to identify winners and jettison mediocre divisions in this context.

In most industries, the firms that will prove to be the most competitive producers in North America will be a combination of U.S., Canadian and foreign-owned companies. As such, foreign direct investment has a key role to play in U.S. and Canadian industrial progress. It is the way North America can access the best product and process technologies.[36] In virtually all industries, highly mobile corporate capital is gravitating to the most appropriate locations for product development, production and marketing, as defined by the availability of high quality, less mobile human and natural resources and by national industrial and trade policies.

For a small country such as Canada, these trends make meaningful interactions between industrial policy makers and its corporate community difficult and delicate. Further exacerbating the complexity of Canadian policy choices, though, are American responses to U.S. technological dependency.

An American Industrial Policy?

The U.S. private sector increasingly recognizes the need to band together to overcome the barriers to precompetitive research. As noted above, such research often requires large groups of companies from a wide range of industries to spread high costs and more fully appropriate the downstream commercial benefits. For example, the membership of Sematech is much broader than semiconductors manufacturers—it includes Boeing, Minnesota Mining and Manufacturing, General Electric, and Eastman Kodak.

In many ways, precompetitive research is coming to be viewed as a public good, much like but distinct from basic scientific research. Industry leaders and science policy advocates within the Congress and federal agencies view it as a critical part of the infrastructure necessary to support new products and process R & D and national competitiveness in high-technology industries.

In 1983, the Microelectronics & Computer Technology Corporation was established by 21 U.S. companies, with each contributing in $1.5 billion a year, to counter Japanese gains in fifth generation computer technology. In 1986, the U.S. Department of Commerce took the lead in establishing Sematech, a consortium of 14 companies seeking to develop advanced chip-making technology with the help of $200 million in Pentagon contracts.[37] Also in 1986, the U.S. government established the National Center for Manufacturing Sciences (NCMS) to help bolster the machine tools industry—the Defense Department provides $5 million annually and this is matched by $45 million in private funds.[38]

Gradually two things happened during the 1980s. First, as evidenced by the proliferation of corporate alliances in product development and process dissemination, American industry lost some of its cultural resistance to banding together. Second, under President Reagan, the U.S. government began taking a more active role, acknowledging the tremendous clout its defence spending could have if more effectively focused. The federal focus shifted, at least in part, from mere support for mission oriented research (e.g., research oriented towards broad societal goals and specific defence needs), which assumes a viable industrial base, to programs that actively seek to assure the maintenance and expansion of a viable industrial base.

Starting in 1985, the U.S. federal government established 18 Engineering Research Centers on university campuses to encourage commercial research and has freed national laboratories to collaborate with industry. This was part of a general effort to encourage greater commercial focus in university research. Also, the federal government awards Small Business Innovation Grants.

At the DARPA, the nerve centre of U.S. defence R & D, officials began approaching the re-establishment and expansion of the civilian DRAMs, semiconductor and microprocessor industries as critical to the American ability to maintain its sophisticated military arsenal. DARPA funds had long supported work in computers, electronics and advanced materials, and it took a highly visible role in overseeing Sematech and in awarding contracts to foster high-definition televisions. Craig Fields, appointed by President Bush to head DARPA in 1989, became a strong advocate of investing DARPA funds in dual-use technologies, and specifically those with both civilian and military applications.

In 1989, the Defense and Energy Departments identified 22 technologies, ranging from gallium arsenide to computer modelling to biotechnology materials and processing, as critical to national security.[39] At the state and local levels several government programs emerged to help small suppliers satisfy the demands from their larger customers that they adopt practices such as just-in-time manufacturing and delivery and statistical quality control.[40]

What did all of this mean? In mid-1989 *Business Week* concluded:

> While there is still no clear policy, over the past eight years Washington has gradually mounted a broad effort to emulate the cooperative success of Japan Inc.[41]

These efforts set off a debate within the Bush Administration over the efficacy of these efforts. In early 1990, advocates of an aggressive U.S. innovation policy, such as Mr. Fields and Commerce Secretary Robert Mosbacher lost out to critics led by Michael Boskin, Richard Darman and John Sununu. Symbolically, funding for HDTV was curtailed and Mr. Fields resigned his post.

Although one can argue that the risks and externalities inherent in precompetitive research may warrant a government role in forming and financing research consortia, conservatives within the Bush Administration see direct involvement with industry as trying to pick winners. However, they endorse government assistance for precompetitive research at universities and national laboratories. The real question boils down to: Where does precompetitive research end and commercial product and process development begin? Is government help necessary to foster industry consortia and an adequate technology infrastructure?

So far, American companies have generally shunned opportunities to band together in projects similar to Sematech without government assistance. Most notably, despite strong leadership from IBM, U.S. Memories—a consortium conceived in 1989 to re-establish U.S. production of DRAMs—failed to attract enough backers.[42]

Nevertheless, sentiments remain strong within the Democrat-controlled Congress and the business community for a more supportive federal role. The Office of Technology Assessment advocates the creation of a civilian DARPA within the Commerce Department to organize and focus federal support for precompetitive research and aid to U.S. industry in responding to Japanese competition.[43]

In early 1990, the Department of Commerce, which continues to be headed by industrial policy advocate Robert Mosbacher, reported that the United States is losing ground in most precompetitive technologies to both Japan and the EC.[44] The Defense Department list of critical technologies closely parallels the Commerce Department civil list,[45] raising the possibility of a national security justification for a movement in policy.

Canadian Interests in a Changed World

As the FTA moves the United States and Canada toward a single market, technological change and global competition are driving adjustments that make the two national economies more similar, more dependent on overseas technology and capital, and less independent of foreign influence.

As Canadian reliance on resource exports and U.S. dominance in knowledge-intensive spheres continues to decline, cross-border competition for investment and jobs in traditional manufacturing activities grows. Access to capital and the best production methods often requires Asian and European investors and management. U.S. and Canadian participation in knowledge-intensive activities frequently requires foreign partners, which may be privately or state owned.

American response to lost industrial and technological supremacy has included more proactive industrial policies and a surprising business acceptance of cooperative ventures and business-government partnerships. As discussed in Chapter 5, the U.S. response to increased foreign ownership has been rather ambivalent. American policies have expanded from the selected use of reactive measures, such as contingent protection in import-impacted industries, to broader actions intended to improve American technological capabilities. The U.S. government is no longer merely accepting the competitive benefits that may flow from its defence R & D programs, national laboratories and university research—it has sought to remove impediments to them. For the time being, though, the Bush Administration has decided to: strictly define basic and precompetitive research qualifying for government aid; not to go beyond removing barriers to the commercial benefits that may flow from federally-funded research; and not to evolve a more aggressive, comprehensive national response to government organized and funded research consortia in Japan and the EC. Nevertheless, pressures within the Congress for a more assertive federal role are growing and support from companies like IBM indicate the issue of more aggressive federal action will crest periodically.

Canadian firms, like other foreign firms, may compete for contracts from DARPA and participate in most other federal and state programs but government funded activities generally must be domiciled in the United States. A drift towards government steering of resources, such as through the creation of a civilian DARPA, could radically alter incentives for U.S., Canadian and offshore firms as to the choice of North American locations for R & D-intensive activities between the United States and Canada.

One of the key motivating factors for Canada in negotiating the FTA was that the threat of U.S. contingent protection was discouraging investment in Canada. However, a much greater threat to the development of Canadian R & D-intensive activities could be posed by a shift in U.S. industrial policies from passive support for high-technology industries to more aggressive American responses to Japanese and EC competition. In framing strategies for follow-on FTA negotiations on subsidies, procurement and other issues, Canadian policy makers should not only consider the threat posed by U.S. contingent protection to the effective application of Canadian industrial and regional policies. They should also consider the consequences of a potentially more aggressive U.S. industrial policy for Canadian industrial opportunities. A discipline on domestic subsidies, for example, could have the effect of limiting Canadian freedom of action to attract the best offshore technology but permit the United States considerable freedom of action in subsidizing the development of U.S. domiciled R & D-intensive industries.

For Canada, the risks associated with aggressive American policies are not new. However, broader U.S. efforts to foster technological competitiveness would represent the kind of significant shift in American practice which in the past has precipitated a major rethinking of Canadian policies towards the United States. In the nearer term, more focused American actions, such as the aggressive use of countervailing duties and state efforts to attract foreign investors, remain most critical for Canada. Taking a longer-term view, the potential bilateral spill-over effects of more *dirigiste* U.S. policies could present Canadian negotiators with complex challenges and choices. These should be a consideration for Canadians as they define objectives for FTA talks on subsidies, procurement and other issues. Chapter 5 will discuss this further.

Notes

1. For a review of recent Japanese and EC initiatives see Sylvia Ostry, *Governments & Corporations in a Shrinking World: Trade and Innovation Policies in the United States, Europe and Japan* (New York: Council on Foreign Relations Press, 1990), pp. 61-75; and Department of Commerce, *Emerging Technologies: A Survey of Technical and Economic Opportunities* (Washington, D.C.: Dept. of Commerce, Technology Administration, 1990), pp. 49-50.

2. Since 1969, these services have generally accounted for 10 to 18 per cent of U.S. current account receipts, and this share has not exhibited a marked upward trend. In 1988, fees and royalties and private business services, two areas once expected to experience dramatic growth, contributed only 2 and 5 per cent of U.S. export earnings, respectively; instead, travel and transportation continued to dominate, accounting for 11 per cent.

3. See The National Commission on Excellence in Education, *A Nation at Risk* (Washington, D.C.: U.S. Government Printing Office, 1983; Secretary of Education [William J. Bennett], *American Education: Making It Work* (Washington, D.C.: U.S. Government Printing Office, 1988).

4. A return by the United States to current account equilibrium would magnify the consequences of these trends in mature industries.

5. Exacerbating the effects of these developments for U.S. industry, Japanese manufacturers appear to have overtaken U.S. firms in many advanced materials such as metals and alloys, high performance ceramics and new semiconductor materials. See Morici, *Reassessing American Competitiveness*, pp. 133-34.

6. These figures include exports of forest products, petroleum and natural gas, minerals, and basic metals.

7. For a more detailed account of the challenges facing Canadian industry see Morici, *The Global Competitive Struggle*, Chapter 7.

8. According to a study by Woods Gundy, Canadian manufacturers enjoyed an 8 per cent labour cost advantage vis-a-vis their U.S. competitors in 1987 and a 4 per cent disadvantage in 1989. See James Rusk, "Canadian Firms Losing Labour Cost Edge," *The Globe and Mail* (June 5, 1990), B-1, B-6.

9. *Bank of Canada Review* (various issues).

10. This is perhaps most significant for negotiations regarding measures protecting intellectual property. Developed and many developing countries are separated widely on the importance they assign to providing incentives for continued innovation. On the one hand, many support enforcing the property rights of inventors and patent holders. At the same time, many also stress the importance they

place on rapid dissemination of "western technology" and the interests of poorer consumers in developing countries with regard to items such as pharmaceuticals.

11. Specifically, major U.S. trading partners see governments as having important roles to play in helping private firms decipher and respond to market signals. Moreover, the contrast between Japanese and U.S. competitive performance has damaged the credibility of American exhortations about the efficacy of nonintervention, as has increasing U.S. reliance on managed trade agreements in industries such as steel and semiconductors, growing American inclinations to support high-technology industries, the tightening of U.S. trade remedy laws, and the use of Super 301 of the Trade Act of 1988.

12. See Peter Morici, "Implications for U.S. Policy," in *Making Free Trade Work: The Canada-U.S. Agreement* (New York: Council on Foreign Relations, 1990), Chapter 6.

13. See Richard I. Kirkland, Jr., "Merger Mania Is Sweeping Europe," *Fortune* (December 19, 1989), pp. 157-167.

14. Peter Drysdale and Ross Garnaut, "A Pacific Free Trade Area?" in Jeffrey Schott (ed.), *Free Trade Areas and U.S. Trade Policy* (Washington, D.C.: Institute of International Economics, 1989), p. 235.

15. Carla Rapoport, "Japan's Growing Global Reach," *Fortune* (May 22, 1989), pp. 48-56.

16. For example, see Lawrence Surtrees, "Group Vies to Let Planes Phone Home," *The Globe and Mail* (September 4, 1989), p. B-1 and William C. Symonds, "American Cable Is Lassoing Foreign Markets," *Business Week* (August 14, 1989) pp. 70-71.

17. A critical reason behind Japanese joint ventures with U.S. financial institutions is to gain access to high technology investment skills. See Michael R. Sesit and James A. White, "Japanese Firms Have Yen for U.S. High-Tech Investment Skills," *The Wall Street Journal* (July 11, 1989), pp. C-1, C-25.

18. See Leon Muszynski and David Wolfe, "New Technology and Training: Lessons from Abroad," *Canadian Public Policy*, Vol. XV, No. 3 (September 1989), pp. 248-249; and Morici, *Reassessing American Competitiveness*, pp. 123-127.

19. Nicholas Valery, "Factory of the Future," *The Economist* (May 30, 1987).

20. Ronald Henkoff, "What Motorola Learns from Japan," *Fortune* (April 24, 1989), pp. 157-168.

21. For a discussion of the Westinghouse approach, see Chester A. Sadlow, *Looking Ahead* (Summer 1987), pp. 6-11.

22. Economic Council of Canada, *Innovation and Jobs in Canada* (Ottawa: Supply and Services Canada, 1987), p. 75.

23. Maryellen F. Kelley and Harvey Brooks, *The State of Computerized Automation in U.S. Manufacturing* (Cambridge, Mass.: Center for Business and Government, John F. Kennedy School of Government, 1988), p. 3. Also, anecdotal evidence supports these findings. See Joel Dreyfuss, "Shaping up Your Suppliers," *Fortune* (April 10, 1989), pp. 116-122.

24. Computer-assisted automation facilitates economies of scope by making it possible to achieve large volumes through the production of a wide range of small batch, phase-in and phase-out products.

25. Jeremy Main, "How to Go Global—and Why?" *Fortune* (August 28, 1989), p. 70.

26. Joseph Weber and Susan Benway, "Filling Bristol-Myers' Prescription," *Business Week* (August 14, 1989), p. 81.

27. J. Michael Geringer and Patrick Woodcock, "Ownership and Control of Canadian Joint Ventures," *Business Quarterly* (Summer 1989), pp. 97-105.

28. Louis Kraar, "Your Rivals Can Be Your Best Allies," *Fortune* (March 27, 1989), p. 68.

29. "Back to Basics: Spreading the Risks," *Business Week* (Special Issue, 1989), p. 64.

30. Chuck Hawkins, "Is Paul Stern Tough Enough to Toughen Up Northern Telecom?" *Business Week* (August 14, 1989), p. 85.

31. Ken Romain, "Canadair and Indonesia Plane Project," *The Globe and Mail* (December 18, 1989), p. B-3.

32. Alex Taylor, III, "The Tasks Facing General Motors," *Fortune* (March 13, 1989), p. 53.

33. Ronald Henkoff, "What Motorola Learns from Japan," p. 168.

34. See Jacob M. Schlesinger, "IBM Toshiba to Produce Screens Jointly," *The Wall Street Journal* (August 31, 1989), p. B-5.

35. These differences emanate from such intangibles as the quality of corporate leadership, the flexibility of unions, the tone of labour-management relations, the ability to cooperate and influence government policy makers, the adaptability of corporate cultures, the size and strength of overseas presence, and the quality of foreign affiliates and joint venture partners.

36. Even if U.S., European and Japanese current accounts were in equilibrium, international capital markets were perfect, and the costs and availability of debt and equity financing varied little among countries, foreign direct investment would play a critical role in the industrial adjustment process underway in North America. Foreign companies will locate where the environment for production is most attractive and where there are large markets, especially if access is threatened. Factor prices and market access remain key in determining where plants are located, but the ability to cope with modern technology—i.e., access to mobile R & D capital and expertise—are critical for determining who owns and manages them. Massive U.S. current account deficits and Japanese surpluses, concerns about future American protectionist actions, and the potential for large movements in the U.S. dollar only serve to magnify the consequences of these trends.

37. "Innovation in America: Washington Inc.," *Business Week* (Special Issue, 1989), p. 40.

38. *Economic Report of the President* (Washington, D.C.: U.S. Government Printing Office, 1989), pp. 248-249.

39. See Martin Tolchin, "Crucial Technologies: 22 Make the U.S. List," *The New York Times* (March 17, 1989), pp. D-1 and D-3; and Department of Defense, "Critical Technologies Plan" (Washington, D.C.: mimeo., submitted to the Committees on Armed Services, United States Congress, March 15, 1989).

40. These include the Cleveland Advanced Manufacturing Program, Ohio's Thomas Edison Program, the National Institute of Standards regional manufacturing centres, and the Wichita Kansas and Sedgwick County (WI/SE) Partnership for Growth. The Cleveland Advanced Manufacturing Program provides free assessments of manufacturing processes and is one of nine technology centres established under Ohio's Thomas Edison Program.
     Also, the National Institute of Standards has established regional manufacturing technology centres in Cleveland, Troy, New York and Columbia, South Carolina. The WI/SE Partnership for Growth brings together resources from government, the private sector and Wichita State's Institute for Aviation Research and Composite Materials Laboratory to help small suppliers of companies such as Cessna, Beech Aircraft, Gates Learjet, Boeing, and others implement state of the art computer-automated manufacturing systems. In Pennsylvania, the state government and the private sector are raising $60 million to establish technology centres that would help small manufacturers with new technology, management and marketing. See Joel Dreyfuss, "Shaping Up Your Suppliers," *Fortune* (April 10, 1989), pp. 116-122.

41. "Innovation in America,", pp. 40-41.

42. Stephen Kreider Yoder, "U.S. Memories, Already Fading, Dies," *The Wall Street Journal* (January 16, 1990), B-1 and B-9.

43. Office of Technology Assessment, *Making Things Better: Competing in Manufacturing* (Washington, D.C.: U.S. Government Printing Office, 1990).

44. Department of Commerce, *Emerging Technologies: A Survey of Technical and Economic Opportunities*, (Spring 1990), p. xiii.

45. U.S. Department of Defense, *Critical Technologies Plan* (Washington, D.C.: March 15, 1990); Department of Commerce, *Emerging Technologies*, p. 45.

Chapter 5

National Policies, the Free Trade Agreement and Bilateral Relations

The trends in comparative advantages, technology and the global trading system discussed in Chapter 4 are driving industrial adjustment and national policy responses in North America. These have important consequences for bilateral relations and the effective evolution of the Canada-U.S. Free Trade Agreement.

Industrial Adjustments and Bilateral Relations

The developments in global competition, technology and business practices that are most important to bilateral relations and the future of the FTA can be divided into five groups.

First, changes in comparative advantages and technology are pushing U.S. and Canadian industries towards greater emphasis on mature manufacturing activities. Specifically, the United States has ceded leadership in many high-technology activities to Japanese and other foreign competitors. Canada now relies less on natural resource-based exports.

Second, the emergence of ever more powerful communications/information and manufacturing technologies are propelling a massive retooling of industry in the advanced industrial economies. More and more, Japan is setting the pace of change and defining its character in manufacturing. In industries where

111

Japan has overtaken western rivals, its aggressive assault on global markets, through exports and foreign investment, dictates the rate at which North American and European firms must invest in and master new technologies if they are to remain viable without protection. Ultimately, it is competition from Japan and the East Asian newly industrializing countries that compels the rationalization and modernization of Canadian industry—this is the team to beat in the rich American market.

Third, firms are being compelled to globalize operations and forge alliances in "core" business activities to spread soaring product development costs, absorb new manufacturing technologies and acquire international marketing capabilities. The rising cost of generic precompetitive research requires diverse industry consortia and perhaps government assistance to adequately spread costs, risks and benefits.

Fourth, as the Uruguay Round moves to an end, businesses exhibit caution with regard to the prospect for improved international market access. Along with the consolidation of trading areas in Europe, North America and Asia and the proliferation of government support for R & D, this prospect further motivates multinational corporations (MNCs) to disperse globally production, central management functions and R & D to assure understanding of, access to and favourable treatment in each regional market.

Fifth, there are enormous variations among North American and foreign companies in their abilities to cope with this fluid competitive environment. In many U.S./Canadian markets, the most capable firms are a combination of traditional indigenous suppliers and foreign companies who now find it profitable to set up production in North America, setting the stage for intense binational competition among communities to keep and attract competitive employers.

Cross-Border Tensions in Mature Industries

For communities dependent on one or a few employers in mature industries, an improved environment for competitive production in North America will not necessarily translate into benefits for local workers or other immobile resources. If major employers are not among the more agile North American competitors or if new plants are required to sustain or regain competitiveness, communities could still suffer plant closures and substantial disruptions in their local economies and labour markets.

There are situations in which market opportunities for North American producers are shrinking or growing only slowly, but the industry in Canada or the United States is in a better position to prosper. Examples include Canadian steel and basic nonferrous metals and U.S. household furniture. Alternatively, there are situations in which adequate market opportunities are emerging for North American-based production, but a rearrangement of the competitive pecking order among U.S., Canadian and foreign-owned companies sets off intense competition for market shares. As foreign-owned companies establish new facilities and long-established North American suppliers modernize, excess capacity becomes apparent and communities compete to attract or keep employers. An important illustration of this phenomenon has been the displacement of Chrysler and General Motor's shares of North American production by Japanese and Korean subsidiaries and the competition among states, provinces and communities to keep and attract major automotive assembly and components plants.

State and provincial governments will continue to face strong political pressures to assist communities in attracting and keeping employers. Subnational government subsidies may have little impact on corporate decisions to locate or maintain production in North America, and often their greatest consequences are for the division of local tax burdens between highly mobile corporate resources and relatively immobile local resources. Nevertheless, the binational character of this competitive subsidization places significant political constraints on the abilities of Washington and Ottawa to bring this ruinous competition under control. Plainly, it is quite difficult for Ottawa to lobby Ontario about the long-term costs of incentives offered to an Asian automotive producer if the principal competition comes from Michigan or Tennessee.

Adjustment and political pressures are likely to be most acute during periods of slow growth or recession, and producers in mature industries have repeatedly displayed their inclination to seek import relief through safeguard actions, voluntary restraint agreements, dumping laws, or whatever means may be at hand to achieve politically what they have failed to win in the market-place.

With three-quarters of its exports going to the United States, the effectiveness of FTA provisions that could shelter Canadian producers from the full force of U.S. safeguard and grey-area actions and the abuse of U.S. trade-remedy laws will be critical for Canada. The vulnerability of the U.S. nonferrous metals sector to global competitive pressures, technological change and Canadian competitive advantages make it a likely stage for this drama. Alternatively, should the steel voluntary restraint agreements actually end in 1992, Canadian mills could join U.S. mini-mills in turning up the heat on U.S. integrated producers.

Should the U.S. industries seek global safeguard actions, under the FTA, Canadian exports to the United States may not be reduced "below the trend of imports over a reasonable base period with allowance for growth."[1] With regard to grey-area actions, Canadian officials believe this provision provides similar shelter from future U.S. programs of voluntary restraint agreements, because it is the threat of safeguard actions that often prompts exporters to accept voluntary restraint agreements (VRAs). This was the case for Canadian steel in 1984. However, since VRAs were not explicitly mentioned in FTA Article 1102, Richardson has warned that U.S. officials might argue that such logic does not apply.[2] In response, Canadian officials would argue that the FTA precludes any restrictions on exports which would "enforce" "voluntary" export restraints.

Even within the context of a straightforward GATT Article XIX action, defining a limit on Canadian exports consistent with "the trend of imports over a reasonable base period" will prove difficult. Another politically hot adjustment problem involving Canadian exporters, such as could occur in nonferrous metals, could precipitate a crisis for the FTA. If Canadians perceive FTA protections as inadequate, future progress in the follow-on nego-tiations under the agreement could be jeopardized. This issue needs to be clarified and, if necessary, addressed before an unmanageable problem surfaces.

Bringing subsidies under effective control is an equally complicated problem for many reasons. For example, although the U.S. government has expressed strong interest in achieving some international discipline over subsidies, domestic political pressures are growing for federal assistance to industry to help counter foreign competition and industrial policies. An agreement with Canada would result in a discipline covering 100 per cent of U.S. subsidies in exchange for a discipline on subsidies in a country accounting for only 20 per cent of U.S. trade.

This issue would become particularly troublesome for the U.S. federal government should it expand the scope of its assistance to high-technology industries through such vehicles as the National Center for Manufacturing Sciences, Defense Advanced Research Projects Agency (DARPA) or a proposed civilian DARPA. Such programs impart benefits through procurement, technical assistance and research support, raising the whole issue of what concepts of actionable trade distorting subsidies can the U.S. and Canadian governments accept. There is also the issue of how to treat defence purchases, other public procurement, R & D support, regional aids, and state and provincial programs.

These are familiar problems. Even more vexing, though, this discussion illustrates that managed trade and subsidies often have the same origins—globally imposed structural adjustment—and they can have the same binational predatory effects in contracting or restructuring industries. It also illustrates the difficulties of addressing subsidies separately from adjustment, managed trade, procurement and other non-tariff issues. Yet FTA Chapter 19 requires negotiators to do just that.

Investment- and Technology-Related Issues

The globalization of competition, corporate functions and business collaboration raises several issues for U.S. policy makers that their Canadian counterparts have had to grapple with for more than a generation, as well as some new ones for Canada.

The dispersion of key corporate functions between North America and Europe will likely result in a cross-Atlantic swapping of R & D, marketing and management responsibilities, and government influence on business decisions. For Canada, though, the flow of core corporate functions and public influence could prove less symmetrical—it could become decidedly north to south and west to east. Canadian concerns are quite understandable, for example, that Northern Telecom may shed its Canadian identity[3] as it further internationalizes operations. Similar outcomes could occur as small Canadian firms enter into alliances with or are merged into the operations of larger foreign competitors. Such considerations contributed to Investment Canada's concerns regarding Merieux's acquisition of Connaught Laboratories.[4] While the Canadian government can influence this process by seeking, for example, world product mandates, R & D commitments and other undertakings from foreign investors, important risks are inherent in such approaches and delicate analysis and action are required to maximize Canadian interests.

Turning to the United States, the globalization of markets and production requires that domestic production in many important industries, ranging from automobiles to zinc, have some component of foreign involvement. Along with more international corporate alliances and slipping American leadership in many high-technology spheres, this trend requires, by first principles, greater American dependence on foreign capital and technology. Many Americans are displaying the same kind of discomfort with foreign influence as did Canadians with regard to American influence in the 1970s and early 1980s.

To date, U.S. reactions to dependency have been a mixture of ambivalence and action. The administration continues to champion an open door for foreign investment and technology, and it campaigns for the inclusion of investment policies and disciplines on other industrial policies under the GATT umbrella. Meanwhile, the administration has implemented national security screening of acquisitions of U.S. assets by foreign companies as required by the 1988 Trade Act and it has taken proactive steps to reorient federally-funded R & D towards greater commercial benefits. The Congress has flirted with more stringent monitoring of foreign subsidiaries and is studying the efficacy of a more focused national science and technology policy.

Agitation in Congress about foreign investment raises the spectre of general screening—the birth of an "Investment America" that might look more like Canada's old Foreign Investment Review Agency than Investment Canada. Should such an Investment America emerge, the FTA clearly guarantees Canadian firms exemption from general screening. Moreover, Canada could become more attractive to Asian and European MNCs as a production platform for the rich American market. However, careful management of Canada's domestic fiscal affairs and foreign investment policies would be critical. Although an Investment America would impose certain costs on foreign subsidiaries in the United States, Canada's taxes and its own federal and provincial expectations for foreign firms—e.g., world product mandates, Canadian-based R & D and local sourcing—could negate the advantages of locating in Canada. Clearly, in North America, as in Europe, offshore investment will flow to the locations with the most hospitable policies and attractive local resources.

An increase in the scope of U.S. federal and state involvement in commercial R & D and the implementation of advanced technologies, could have both positive and negative consequences for Canada. An aggressive and well-funded American industrial policy could impart substantial benefits to Canadian MNCs, like Northern Telecom, having significant manufacturing and R & D activities domiciled in the United States. Likewise, strengthening the technological capabilities of American companies with operations in both countries would create competitive benefits for Canada. However, an aggressive expansion of U.S. commercial R & D incentives could encourage Canadian firms to shift their R & D activities to the United States. It could also cause offshore investors to see Canada as a good location for fabrication and assembly plants to service the combined U.S./Canadian market, but to see the United States as a preferred location for R & D and innovative manufacturing activities.

The trend towards greater cooperation among U.S. companies in product development, manufacturing and marketing, would be a big plus for Canadian firms *if* they are permitted to participate. For strictly private efforts this may not prove to be as difficult as it sounds. Increasingly, private joint ventures and alliances are international in scope, and the participation of Canadian firms will be determined by the expertise Canadians can bring to the enterprise.

Turning to large industry consortia, the Microelectronics & Computer Technology Corporation, being generally private, has opened up to Canadian firms in the wake of the FTA.[5] However, Sematech being financed and directed by DARPA, is open only to foreign firms undertaking contracted work in the United States. Should such commercially motivated government programs increase in number, Canadian firms could be put at considerable disadvantage. In the best of times, the Canadian government has not had the funds, even in proportion to its population and GNP, to finance the scope of R & D efforts that Washington can bankroll, and the late 1980s/early 1990s are not the best of times.

A principal motivation for Canada in seeking a free trade agreement with the United States was to free firms investing in Canada from the risk that 90 per cent of their North American sales could be disrupted or penalized by a U.S. trade action. To the extent that the FTA satisfies this central Canadian concern, either through the provisions of FTA Chapter 19 or in follow-on negotiations, this could prove to be a hollow victory for Canada. An American industrial policy could attract R & D activities and innovative manufacturing to the United States and leave to Canada more routine and less sophisticated fabrication and assembly activities. In this way, such an American industrial policy could have the same kinds of negative consequences for the structure of Canadian manufacturing in the 1990s as did U.S. and European tariffs that escalated with the stage of processing and fabrication in the 1950s and 1960s.

Moreover, there is no guarantee that U.S. policy makers would not muck up an American industrial policy, weakening North American competitiveness more than strengthening it. Although the principal barrier to an American industrial policy seems to be eroding—i.e., cultural opposition within the American business community—European and Japanese experiences with industrial policies, as well as American forays into urban development and agriculture, indicate a wide range of outcomes is possible.

Prospects for the Free Trade Agreement

In assessing the FTA's prospects in this fluid environment, it is important to recognize that many of the agreement's key provisions are general; their full effects will only become apparent as problems arise and with follow-on negotiations. Significant in this regard are discussions on subsidies and related measures, the harmonization issues associated with practices such as product standards and services,[6] and the conduct of dispute settlement.

Subsidies, Procurement, Managed Trade, and Adjustment

One of the salient features of the industrial restructuring and national policy responses described above is that subsidies, managed trade, procurement, and the political problems associated with business and labour adjustments have become tightly intertwined issues.

In the competition among firms for market shares, mastery of technology has become crucial. Corporate survival requires the ability to finance and manage product development, effectively implement new manufacturing processes, and spread costs and reach markets through global operations and alliances.

In the competition among countries and communities for plants and jobs, there are essentially two kinds of resources:

- mobile corporate resources—the capital, managerial talent and technical personnel that are the international conduits of new products and processes;

- relatively immobile local resources—regionally-based labour and public infrastructure.

Resource endowments, and specifically the availability and quality of labour and public infrastructure, still play a central role in determining where products are developed and made. However, corporations can take their capital and technology to the locations that offer the most attractive labour and infrastructure as evaluated in terms of both quality and price.

In the 1960s and 1970s, most major industrial adjustments were imposed by competition from lower cost imports in mature manufacturing and resource industries. U.S. and Canadian governments responded by managing trade and offering subsidies, which reduced or offset national or regional cost disadvantages and tempered labour market and community adjustments.

In the 1990s, with revolutions in manufacturing and information technologies dramatically reducing the number of highly-paid workers and managers required in many industrial activities and North American firms varying so much in their abilities to manage technology, labour and community adjustment are just as ubiquitous in North American industries with good competitive prospects as in those burdened by structural cost disadvantages. National, state and provincial governments have responded with programs to improve the performance of domestically-based companies (e.g., various public R & D and technical assistance programs) and to attract competent foreign investment. Similarly, governments have sought to make local labour and public infrastructure more attractive to domestic and foreign corporate investors.

To protect their tax bases and support the real and psychic incomes of local workers, local governments make special efforts to keep and attract certain employers. Some employers are perceived as better than others, and many workers, especially blue-and grey-collar workers, are reluctant to relocate. Local governments offer tax benefits, specially-tailored training programs and infra-structure projects, and other benefits. They help marshal political pressure on federal, state and provincial governments to assist in financing these efforts and to augment the market opportunities of local employers through procurement preferences and managed trade.

Clearly, subsidies, procurement and managed trade are frequently imperfect substitutes in the hands of industrial policy makers. Efforts to control the bilateral predatory effects of any one of these practices alone will likely lead to the compensating use of others. Moreover, with sentiments in Washington growing for a more active government role in addressing the Japanese challenge and with North American communities engaged in intense competition to attract employers, it is doubtful that Washington or Ottawa could muster the political capital to forsake completely these practices, especially within the context of a bilateral accord. Complete disciplines would have to be achieved through the GATT where sweeping progress is unlikely. With the United States and Canada moving towards a single market in virtually all indus-tries, the real challenge for FTA negotiators will be to find ways to contain the bilateral predatory effects of subsidies, procurement and managed trade as a group, building on whatever progress the Uruguay Round may yet achieve.

Focusing on *subsidies*, Horlick and Steger have offered a proposal that would build on the practices the two governments could agree to while recognizing the limits of bilateral achieve-ment. Briefly, they propose the establishment of a structure or committee of officials from the two governments to review proposed and existing programs against lists of prohibited and permissible subsidies. Practices found to be in the prohibited category, or direct subsidies on neither the prohibited or permissible list but imparting benefits above an agreed upon amount, say "X" per cent, if not removed, would be subject to border measures similar to countervailing duties without an injury test. Indirect subsidies falling in the middle ground would be permitted but would continue to be countervailable subject to a more rigorous injury test than is currently applied.

Horlick and Steger also make several recommendations to reduce the incidence and cost of countervailing duty cases including: consultations prior to initiating investigations; at the outset of an investigation, requiring a binational committee to determine the sufficiency of evidence and provide an advisory opinion on the effects of a subsidy; and more rigorous standing requirements and definitions of injury.[7]

This proposal has the merits of seeking some limits on the cross-border effects of subsidies, while granting both governments continued flexibility to undertake transparent and reasonably moderate industrial policies (i.e., direct aid below "X" per cent) and guaranteeing Canada safe harbour for social and cultural programs. This approach offers the Congress the prospect of some discipline over direct Canadian industrial aids, which it perceives to be more pervasive than American aids, in exchange for agreeing to some reforms sought by Canadians in the application of countervailing duties.[8]

Initially, the prohibited and permissible lists would be short, including items such as clear export subsidies on the one hand, and social programs, support for cultural industries and health care on the other. Important in these discussions would be the classification of benefits provided through U.S. defence procurement. For example, the United States and Canada might agree to shelter R & D programs from whatever discipline emerges. However, should U.S. government efforts to bolster American technology continue to expand, a green light for comparable Canadian efforts might not prove enough for Canada. This raises the whole issue of Canadian access to U.S. *procurement*.

Should Washington shift the focus of its general R & D support and defence procurement towards greater commercial benefits and the pursuit of specific industrial development objectives, the best strategy for Ottawa may be to seek national treatment for Canadian firms for non-defence projects, such as Sematech, and for defence projects having some commercial objectives and spill-overs. With regard to efforts to ensure an adequate defence industrial base, simply put, such national treatment would require the United States to recognize Canadian facilities as secure and reliable elements of that base. There is clear precedent for this approach.[9]

Identifying defence expenditures with significant commercial spill-overs, and therefore the potential to negatively influence Canadian industrial development through exports or import substitution, could prove difficult. Nevertheless, it is an issue that has attracted the attention of Canadian officials. In November 1989, chief Canadian negotiator Tony Halliday, in testimony before the House of Commons Standing Committee on External Affairs and International Trade stated:

> We want to look at the types of programs that are available within the Department of Defense to see to what extent those programs can be categorized as having a defence objective or having spill-overs into the commercial sector, which we would regard as conferring subsidies going beyond the needs of United States defence institutions.[10]

Such national treatment of Canadian firms in the United States would require similar treatment for American firms in Canada. Considering Canadian sensitivities about some U.S. defence projects, such an exchange of national treatment in research efforts could raise a panoply of difficult political issues for Ottawa.

Although these problems are complex, Canada cannot afford to have its indigenous firms, especially small- and medium-sized firms, faced with the choice of locating facilities in the United States or being cut out of an aggressive American industrial policy should one emerge. Its policy makers should follow closely proposals in the United States for a national science and technology policy and the general commercialization of defence, national laboratory and university research. These developments should be of central concern to Canadian officials as they prepare for negotiations on subsidies and government procurement under the FTA.

Beyond expanding the scope of federal purchases covered by the FTA procurement chapter, the other major procurement issue is state and provincial discrimination. This raises the familiar question of the political and constitutional abilities of the two federal governments to bind the states and provinces to the disciplines of a trade agreement. Washington and Ottawa frequently skirted this issue in the FTA by exempting state and provincial practices from key provisions of the agreement such as the product standards and procurement chapters. Perhaps the best tack here would be to accept half a loaf—seek agreement from the states (provinces) to treat the provinces (states) in the same fashion as they do other states (provinces).[11] Since the primary purpose of state and provincial procurement discrimination is to bestow benefits on local businesses and workers, such national treatment in extra-state/provincial purchases should not upset state and provincial sensitivities too much. The two federal governments could then work in tandem to eliminate interstate and interprovincial barriers.

A second binational committee, composed of officials from the two federal executives, such as the one suggested above for subsidies disputes or the one below for the supervision of safeguards, could advise the Canada-United States Trade Commission concerning which federal programs would be subject to the new procurement arrangement's national treatment provisions. This committee could also have representation from the governors and premiers to oversee the provisions applying to state and provincial practices.

Focusing on *safeguards and grey-area measures*, which often emerge from the threat of safeguard actions, Richardson has proposed redefining domestic producers eligible for temporary protection to include only immobile resources (e.g., workers and small firms). He also suggests establishing a binational committee—an arms-length agent—to monitor and help manage bilateral safeguard actions. His ideas have the merit of focusing assistance on regionally-based blue- and grey-collar workers—the workers who are generally most sharply affected by imports and form the core voting blocks behind industry efforts to obtain protection. Large domestic corporations can spread risks through global operations.[12] In any case, the foreign competitors of large domestic companies seeking import relief can avoid many of the effects of safeguard and grey-area measures by reallocating production through their global investment networks—consider, for example, the ultimate outcome of voluntary restraint agreements on Japanese automotive exports.

The binational advisory committee on safeguards could be composed of several senior ministers from the two federal executives (for example Treasury, State, External Affairs, and Finance) or private citizens representing them whose incumbency would correspond to the mandates of their president or prime minister. The committee on safeguards would report and be available to the Canada-United States Trade Commission. Following an injury finding by the International Trade Commission or the International Trade Tribunal and in the event the U.S. or Canadian government considered a safeguard action, the committee would analyze alternative relief measures with regard to their likely impacts on the industry in both countries and publish its findings. When either government notified the other of its intention to implement a safeguard action, or institute a program on grey-area measures, the committee could offer advisory opinion to aid the binational consultations required by Article 1102.

Such a process could provide the external discipline necessary for the two governments to resist permanent protection. Along with the emphasis on regionally-based resources, such a process could encourage the use of positive measures such as severance bonuses for workers and small firms, retraining and relocation assistance for workers, technical assistance for small firms, and temporary aid to local governments for maintaining essential public services. The choice of such actions, as alternatives to tariffs, quotas and grey-area actions, are consistent with presidential authority under Section 201 of the U.S. Trade Act of 1974. Emphasis on meaningful assistance to regionally-based resources could help diffuse political pressures on the two federal executives and on the two trade ministers who comprise the Canada-United States Trade Commission.

Efforts to encourage positive adjustment, such as aids to help small businesses modernize or assistance to local governments seeking new employers, could easily run afoul of a subsidies discipline or inspire petitions for countervailing duties. In the end, it may prove useful to combine the functions of the committees proposed into one committee for the implementation of agreements covering subsidies, procurement, and safeguards. Such a binational committee would clearly have a broad mandate and could be supported by a group of designated technical experts within the two governments. Such a group could provide joint analysis of relevant domestic production and trade data and archive the findings and recommendations of the committee.

A single, permanent committee with responsibilities for advising the Canada-United States Trade Commission on issues pertaining to subsidies, procurement and managed trade would be well positioned to evaluate specific policies under investigation in terms of their relationship to other programs and practices benefiting the industry in question. For example, the scope of adjustment benefits for workers and severance bonuses for smaller firms could be a consideration in evaluating a proposed safeguard action or a modernization subsidy to larger companies.

In addition to addressing problems as they arose, the committee, being a permanent body, could examine adjustment issues in industries selected by the Trade Commission or selected by the committee itself. If the committee could identify problem areas before they appeared, joint approaches to adjustment in troubled industries might evolve. More likely and more importantly, such processes could help Canada and the United States avoid adjustment programs that work at cross-purposes and engage in harmful, counterproductive binational predation. With so many industries organized on a binational basis (e.g., automobiles and aerospace) facing slow growing or declining markets or tough offshore competition (e.g., nonferrous metals and electronics) or engaged in fierce intraregional rivalries (e.g., the East and West Coast fisheries), joint study could help avoid conflicts and encourage mutually supportive regional and industrial policies.

Needless to say, a more economically autonomous Quebec could greatly complicate efforts to achieve progress on issues such as subsidies, procurement and managed trade, as well as adjustment issues generally. For example, what kind of representation would Quebec want either through Ottawa or directly for itself in existing bilateral structures or of the kind proposed above? Quebec might find that Washington would oppose independent representation for Quebec, owing to concerns about giving Canada two votes. Such issues can be finessed.

What cannot be finessed, though, would be the more varied Canadian interpretations of and aspirations for the FTA that would become relevant for negotiations with the United States. If Quebec became more assertive in its demands on Ottawa in defining negotiating positions, the other provinces would likely follow. In the future, Washington might find Ottawa even more constrained by its need to consult with and accommodate the provinces than during the 1986-88 negotiations.

These general concerns regarding the status of Quebec apply to most FTA issues in addition to subsidies, procurement, managed trade, and harmonization issues, to which we now turn.

Harmonization Issues

Along with subsidies and managed trade, the harmonization of domestic policies to achieve some progress on non-tariff issues such as dumping, product standards, intellectual property rights, investment performance requirements, and services are key issues on the Uruguay Round, European Community 1992 and FTA agendas. Such harmonization frequently entails bridging major, culturally-based differences in national economic and legal institutions and some sacrifice of sovereignty over some levers of national policies.

Owing to concerns about the scope of American influence and political, economic and cultural sovereignty, Canadians prefer the GATT as a forum to address these issues. However, should the Uruguay Round fail to provide Canada with the same scope of access to its principal markets as smaller European countries will enjoy in the European Community after completion of the 1992 program, bilateral negotiations under the FTA will become critically important for the competitiveness of Canadian industry. This would greatly increase pressures on Canada to harmonize its policies and practices with those of the United States.

Two observations are important here. First, it would be slow progress in the GATT and European integration that would pressure Canada to solidify and expand its access to U.S. markets. The FTA provides Canada with the means to achieve these ends, but it is not the force motivating this process. Second, many non-tariff barriers to U.S.-Canadian trade, such as those imposed by product standards and the regulation of business services, are neither as pervasive nor typically cumbersome as those in Europe prior to 1992. The processes of reducing the impediments to trade between two very similar countries like the United States and Canada require neither the same degree of harmonization nor the ceding of sovereign control over domestic policy as do comparable efforts to liberalize trade among the more diverse 12 EC member states. For example, whereas in Europe common floors are required for product standards, in North America all that is likely needed are more compatible approaches to achieving similar national goals. Whereas national treatment of virtually all goods is essential to breaking down the trade barriers imposed by government procurement practices in Europe, a less encompassing, more flexible approach would be workable in a North American regime—more liberal than the GATT Procurement Code but not as comprehensive as the EC 1992 approach.

Dispute Settlement

For the FTA to be an effective framework for managing the commercial relationship, the two governments must abide by the spirit as well as the letter of the agreement. Each government must refrain from overloading the dispute settlement mechanism, for example, by espousing frivolous interpretations of FTA provisions as a means for putting off compliance with the agreement's disciplines or required changes in practices. Similarly, the two governments must make the dispute settlement mechanisms work by promptly negotiating compromises and reaching consensus within the Canada-United States Trade Commission upon receipt of panel reports and by quickly altering national practices as may be required to achieve compliance with panel findings and negotiated settlements.

With regard to the latter, should dispute settlement panels consistently fail to render crisp, clear and decisive findings—specifically, should they fail to either find disputed actions consistent with FTA obligations or fail to identify a clear set of remedial steps—the FTA's dispute settlement procedures may require modification. Should panels consistently seek to split the differences between national positions, as opposed to rigorously and fairly applying FTA and GATT principles, their reports, although generally narrowing the scope of disputes, will not necessarily depoliticize disputes.

In contrast to more decisive findings, panel reports that split the differences will not facilitate effectively the emergence of a body of precedents and interpretations concerning the meaning and subtleties of various provisions of the agreement.

The first Chapter 18 panel report in 1989 on Canadian landing requirements for West Coast salmon and herring, was less than decisive, giving rise to opposing U.S. and Canadian interpretations.[13] The second panel report in 1990, which found U.S. minimum size requirements for imported lobster GATT-consistent, became the focus of strong criticism within the Canadian government.[14] However, both reports instigated a focused period of industry and government discussions that improved understanding of the issues at hand. Also, the future of FTA dispute settlement should not be judged on the basis of two reports.

Many disputes may prove to be too ambiguous for experts to settle clearly and crisply. Panels may only be able to illuminate the requirements of the GATT and the FTA, thereby defining the limits of focused, time-constrained negotiations. Reflecting on the first two panel reports, one observer commented:

> It should be considered quite normal for the parties to take the panel report, sit down and use that as a basis for negotiating a solution.[15]

The Mexico Question

U.S. interest in an agreement with Mexico also poses significant challenges to Canada. During the 1980s, Mexico substantially increased its exports of secondary manufactures to the United States to compensate for lower oil prices, service its external debt and drive its programs of domestic economic reform and trade liberalization. In the process, Mexico's exports to the United States became similar to and competitive with those of Canada,[16] and a Mexico-U.S. trade pact could reduce many benefits of preferential access to the U.S. market Canadian-based manufacturers anticipated from the FTA.

The Parameters of a Mexico-U.S. Trade Agreement

In the near-term, a U.S.-Mexico or a trilateral North American agreement matching the depth of the FTA is not likely to emerge. Labour costs in Mexico and each country's internal political constraints preclude such an ambitious outcome. Yet, as negotiators take the issues addressed by the FTA as a starting point, each side will have a quite different list of items it wishes to withdraw from consideration.

It would clearly serve U.S. interests to achieve long-term guarantees regarding the entry requirements for and the status of American direct investment in Mexico, as well as to obtain concessions regarding energy pricing and supplies. Ultimately, the latter may prove critical to unfettered Mexican access to the U.S. markets in industries such as petrochemicals and primary plastic products. However, overly ambitious concessions to U.S. demands in investment and energy will be difficult for President Salinas to sell at home.

High on Mexico's want list are across the board elimination of tariffs and import restraints and dispute settlement to corral U.S. contingent protection. However, low Mexican wages could devastate some U.S. and Canadian industries and fuel political pressures on President Bush to negotiate long phase-in periods for the elimination of tariffs and other trade barriers in apparel, footwear and basic metals. Similarly, Congress is on record as wanting rigourous safeguard provisions that will permit the reimposition of tariffs for industries severely affected by Mexican competition.

To make a deal that both leaders can sell at home, each side would need concessions from the other on such delicate issues. Both leaders have strong incentives to find elasticity in their negotiating positions to achieve an agreement.

For President Salinas, a free trade pact offers the opportunity to memorialize market-oriented reforms. Future Mexican presidents would be hard pressed to revert to nationalist policies with a restructured industrial sector oriented towards U.S. markets. President Bush cannot afford to let economic reforms fail in

Mexico—the security consequences of a political upheaval there
are unthinkable.

Mexican and U.S. negotiators can finesse difficult issues such
as energy, investment and the vulnerabilities of mature U.S.
industries through phased, yet managed, policy harmonization
and increased market access. Consider, for example, U.S. moves to
grant Mexico greater market shares in steel in 1989 and apparel in
1990, as well as Mexican concessions to foreign investors in
automobiles and other industries in 1989.

Canada's Interests

Canada has a major interest in U.S. negotiations with Mexico.

First, Mexico's fastest growing exports are in the kinds of
products Canada has been banking on under the FTA to supplement its resource sales in the United States. The share of
machinery and transportation equipment in Mexico's U.S.-bound
exports jumped from 21 per cent in 1979 to 43 per cent in 1987.
The latter figure was the same as for Canada. To a considerable
extent, it would appear that Mexico has been achieving its rapid
export growth by bypassing many U.S. import-sensitive industries
and going directly into the kinds of secondary manufacturing
Canadian industrial policy makers have long coveted—e.g., power
generation equipment, telecommunications equipment and electrical equipment.

Giving further impetus to these developments, the Mexican
government is taking far-reaching steps to promote foreign
investment in the automobile industry, one of the last major
Mexican industries with a highly protected domestic market. To
encourage higher volumes and rationalization, the government
has announced plans to increase imports, ease domestic content
requirements and drop restrictions on which models automakers
could produce in Mexico. Nissan has announced a $1 billion
investment program. "We have to invest to get our product up to
international standards," according to Nissan Mexican president
Shoichi Amemiya.[17]

Liberalization of trade in automobiles could give Japanese
automakers the best of all possible worlds—a low-wage export
platform inside the frontier of U.S. contingent protection. In this

and other industries, a U.S.-Mexican agreement, by further integrating Mexico's inexpensive wage base into the cost structures of U.S.-based production, could significantly reduce Canadian competitiveness[18] and some of the benefits anticipated for Canadian business and labour from tariff-free access to the U.S. market.[19]

Mexican exports have not been as substantial or as rapidly growing in the traditional engines of growth of low-wage, industrializing economies—footwear, apparel and steel. Mexico's export drive came after the United States and other industrialized countries had established explicit and implicit policies to limit imports in these categories. A trade agreement with the United States would give Mexico preferential status among developing and industrializing countries, negatively impacting Canadian producers in these and other industries in which Canadian producers are rationalizing to meet increased competition from U.S. imports and to penetrate the larger U.S. market.

After all, the FTA will make the United States the principal market for many rationalizing Canadian manufacturers. Canadian interests could be compromised if Washington unilaterally decides which integrated U.S./Canadian industries will be sheltered from Mexican-based competition through whatever transitional provisions or trade management agreements emerge from negotiations. The best way for Canada to protect these interests is by participating directly in the negotiations.

Second, Canada has a significant stake in ensuring that the arrangements that liberalize U.S.-Mexico trade become increasingly consistent with FTA rules and disciplines as they evolve. Comparable rules for U.S. trade with both Mexico and Canada will better ensure the ability of each to hold the United States to its commitments in areas such as countervailing duties.

In the FTA negotiations, the most significant achievement for Canada may have been to begin the process of subjecting to binational review U.S. actions that might violate GATT-based norms or rescind the benefits anticipated from tariff cuts. A tripartite arrangement would greatly strengthen this gain.

Notes

1. FTA Article 1102.

2. J. David Richardson, "Adjustments and Subsidies," in Peter Morici (ed.), *Making Free Trade Work: The Canada-U.S. Agreement* (New York: Council on Foreign Relations, 1990), Chapter 3.

3. For such an expression of concern see Michael Salter, "Shoot the Moon," *The Globe and Mail Report on Business Magazine* (August 1989), pp. 28-39.

4. Drew Fagan, "Ottawa Threatens to Block Takeover," *The Globe and Mail* (October 14, 1989), pp. A-1 and A-2.

5. Kevin Kelly, "A High-Tech Think Tank Thinks Big Bucks," *Business Week* (September 25, 1989), p. 222.

6. Although FTA Chapter 19 requires the negotiation of substitute rules for both subsidies and dumping, the dumping issue really falls into this category. Negotiators on both sides increasingly see the FTA as creating a single market. It follows logically that for purposes of bilateral trade, the existing dumping regimes should be replaced with a common approach to unfair pricing in a domestic competition policy sense as opposed to a regime premised on international concepts of dumping. This would greatly liberalize trade. For example, many pricing practices for Canadian exports into the United States have been actionable under U.S. dumping law but would not have been actionable under the predatory pricing provisions of U.S. antitrust law if undertaken by U.S. firms.

7. Gary Horlick and Debra Steger, "Subsidies and Countervailing Duties," in Peter Morici (ed.), *Making Free Trade Work: The Canada-U.S. Agreement*, Chapter 4.

8. The reforms in the subsidies/countervailing duty process suggested by Horlick and Steger would limit abuses. Such concessions to Canada, if approved by Congress, would provide an important example of international negotiations imposing positive discipline on U.S. trade policy and insulating U.S. executive branch negotiators and trade officials from protectionist sentiments in the Congress.

9. As discussed in Chapter 2, the United States emerged from World War II as a major importer of ores, concentrates, and basic metals. In the early 1950s, such dependence raised major national security concerns. Subsequently, the U.S. determined that Canadian supplies should be considered as secure and hence were implicitly recognized as part of the U.S. defence industrial base.

10. *Inside U.S. Trade* (November 24, 1989), p. 2.

11. Such a second-order most-favoured-nation concept could be extended to other provisions of the FTA that currently do not apply to the actions of states and provinces.

12. J. David Richardson, "Adjustment and Safeguards," in Peter Morici (ed.), *Making Free Trade Work*, Chapter 3.

13. Madelaine Drohan, "Panel's First Report Leaves Fishy Mess," *The Globe and Mail* (November 21, 1989), pp. C-1 and C-2.

14. See "Lobster Report May Signal FTA Weakness," *Report on Free Trade* (June 4, 1990), pp. 1 and 2; and "Canada May Challenge Lobster Report," *Report on Free Trade* (June 11, 1990), pp. 1 and 2.

15. Madelaine Drohan, "Lobster Industry to Discuss U.S. Ban," *The Globe and Mail* (June 25, 1990), B-2.

16. The rank correlation coefficient of between U.S. imports from Mexico and Canada, as reported in Table A-2, rose from 0.35 in 1979 to 0.51 in 1987.

17. Matt Moffett, "Mexican Debt Pact Hinges on Investment," *The Wall Street Journal* (February 2, 1990), p. A-10.

18. To only a limited degree would FTA's rules of origin deflect U.S. products containing Mexican components from the Canadian market. Outside of textiles and automotive products, which are subject to quite strict rules of origin, the FTA's basic rule is that components be incorporated into other goods or be transformed in ways that are physically or commercially significant. This would not likely pose a major barrier to exports of U.S./Mexican products into Canada.

19. In a paper for the Council on Foreign Relations, Weintraub suggested that the FTA tariff cuts could divert some U.S. imports from Mexico to Canada in machinery, automotive products, petrochemicals, metals, paper products, textiles and apparel and consumer durables. U.S. agreements with Mexico in any of these sectors could reverse these effects. See Sidney Weintraub, "The Impact on Mexico," in Morici (ed.), *Making Free Trade Work*, Chapter 5.

Chapter 6

A New Special Relationship

The Canada-U.S. Free Trade Agreement offers great promise. It has the potential to alter fundamentally the quality and character of the bilateral relationship by liberalizing trade and investment and by providing a flexible and adaptable tool for managing the relationship.

Liberalizing trade and investment was the central goal of the 1986-88 negotiations. The agreement will further integrate the U.S. and Canadian economies and enhance their global competitiveness. Seen in the context of the international global challenges the United States and Canada face, enhanced competitiveness would have been justification enough for the considerable time and effort Washington and Ottawa have devoted and continue to devote to negotiations, consultations and dispute settlement.

A New Partnership?

However, the benefits of the Canada-United States Free Trade Agreement reach much further than removing existing and avoiding new barriers to trade and investment. The FTA has established both processes and a context for better managing the two countries relationship. As the agreement approaches its third anniversary, certain dynamics are beginning to emerge, which if nurtured and sustained could prove critical to the evolution of the bilateral relationship.

The FTA has the potential to forge a new partnership. This can be illustrated by examining the emerging consequences of FTA dispute settlement for trade and industrial policy making in both countries.

At the most basic level, the dispute settlement processes established by Chapters 11, 18 and 19 of the agreement determine whether existing, proposed and newly initiated policies, practices and actions are consistent with the FTA. However, dispute settlement should not be evaluated in terms of a simple box score: How many questionable U.S. and Canadian antidumping or countervailing duty actions are remanded back to national agencies? How many Chapter 18 panel findings are translated directly into revised national policies? Were market shares adequately preserved under a safeguard action? Rather, FTA dispute settlement has the potential to encourage much broader benefits. Three dimensions merit some attention.

First, as discussed in below, Chapters 11 and 19 give the private sectors in each country a special status in the trade policy making processes of the other regarding emergency import actions, antidumping actions and subsidy/countervailing duties.

Prior to the FTA, resource producers, smaller manufacturers and entrepreneurs (hence much of the indigenous Canadian economy) were more vulnerable to risks and uncertainties imposed by the threat of contingent protection than large manufacturers.[1] The new confidence of action afforded these smaller players by Chapters 11 and 19 dispute settlement should encourage investments and engender benefits that easily exceed the benefits generated by the cases actually reviewed by Chapter 19 panels.

Second, as the first two Chapter 18 panel reports illustrated, the disciplines of GATT and FTA consistency may not be applied to many industrial policies as easily as they are to antidumping or subsidy actions. However, Chapter 18 dispute settlement has displayed the capacity to engage the two private sectors in focused and time-constrained processes of conciliation and mediation. This creates the potential for parallel management of natural resources and more harmonious national industrial policies. With so many industries being binational in scope or engaged in tough intraregional competition, such processes have the potential to give rise to complementary national policies.

Third, the fact that statutes affecting bilateral trade may ultimately be subject to bilateral review of uncertain outcome may encourage Washington and Ottawa, and the private sectors that lobby them, to be more preventative in formulating policies and to seek complementary, or at least non-conflicting, approaches to industrial problems.

In some ways, we have already seen movement in this direction in the thinking of the Congress. In 1990, bills were introduced that would require tighter import restraints on textiles and shoes, afford antitrust immunity to joint manufacturing ventures with less than 30 per cent foreign ownership, and impose tougher documentation requirements regarding the safety testing of imported industrial fasteners. In each case, the legislation could have significantly affected Canadian interests even though Canada was not the focus of concern. In each case, legislators, citing the FTA, introduced amendments that afforded special status to Canadian producers.

Such actions pre-empt disputes and offer a clear indication that the Congress recognizes a special status for Canada as a result of the FTA.

Looking to the future, many forces are pressuring Washington to change its approaches to trade and economic development policy. These include the difficulties of achieving substantial progress in the GATT, waning American industrial pre-eminence and the changing context of competition among firms and nations in mature and high-technology industries. Although the policy paths the United States ultimately chooses are difficult to predict, they undoubtedly will have important implications for Canada and will require Canadians to evaluate their own trade and industrial policies.

Far beyond increasing market access in the present, the FTA provides Canadians with processes and a context for negotiating favourable outcomes with the Americans. To the benefit of both countries, the agreement provides a vehicle for achieving smoother bilateral relations.

The GATT System and U.S. Hemispheric Initiatives

A curious irony is at play in the GATT system and the broader global economy. Just as the American view that markets should guide economic development seems to be gaining currency virtually everywhere, American influence is declining. As the notion that national policies must, on the whole, observe the mandates of global markets is increasingly accepted, American exhortations about the efficacy of *laissez faire* national policies are not.

The view that governments can play a vital role in helping industry decipher, and more effectively respond to, market opportunities has been buoyed by Japanese industrial and technological successes. Washington finds itself increasingly at odds with its trading partners who generally embrace broader views of what constitute market-responsive policies. The contrast between Japanese and European Community technology policies and the vision espoused by the Bush Administration for U.S. policy provides a clear example.

American fiscal problems notwithstanding, conflicting views about what constitutes market-responsive policies are at the core of American frustrations with Japan in bilateral talks and with other industrial countries in the GATT. Even if the industrialized countries could agree about what constitutes appropriate market-responsive policies, other obstacles to multilateral progress, discussed in Chapter 4, remain formidable.

All of this has made the creation and expansion of regional arrangements, with the larger EC nations, the United States and Japan at their hubs, convenient supplements or alternatives to the GATT for expanding trade and investment flows. These evolving regional arrangements will increasingly challenge the centrality of the GATT as a vehicle for liberalizing and managing the international commercial system.

Eastern Europe and Latin America

This brings to the fore the critical role that market-oriented reforms in Eastern Europe, Mexico and perhaps other Latin

American countries seem likely to play in emerging trading blocs and in the trade policies of the EC and the United States.

In the 1970s and 1980s, the industrialized nations displayed a persistent reluctance to accept the full economic adjustments implied by industrial progress in the East Asian newly industrializing countries. The expanding scope of industries affected by safeguard actions, antidumping and countervailing duty actions and grey-area measures bears witness to this.

In contrast to industrial progress in East Asia, the EC and the United States have paramount security interests in the success of economic reforms of their eastern and southern neighbours. The EC will have to absorb the exports of Eastern Europe, and the United States places its national interests at great risk if it fails to respond to Mexico's need to expand manufactured exports. EC and U.S. export and investment interests will also lobby for liberal policies.

The more quickly Eastern European and Mexican governments liberalize and transform their economies, the more rapidly the EC and the United States will have to open their markets. In many ways, the pace of liberalization and industrial progress in Eastern Europe and Mexico may drive the pace of liberalization and industrial adjustment in Western Europe and the United States.

On September 25, 1990, President Bush notified the Congress of his intention to enter tripartite trade negotiations with Mexico and Canada. Congress approved fast track negotiations in June 1991. Coupled with the expansion of the EC, the resulting trade and investment flows could create regional blocs encompassing a balance of advanced industrialized economies with capital and technology and industrializing economies with large, trainable and inexpensive workforces.[2]

Given the size of the Eastern European and Mexican labour forces, the magnitude of adjustment challenges imposed on the EC, U.S. and Canadian[3] economies could rival those created by the East Asian NICs in the 1980s.

In the short-run, the growth of Mexican market shares in the United States and Canada could be limited, for example, to a negotiated "X" per cent a year. However, even with safeguards, adjustment pressures on U.S. and Canada as textiles, apparel, steel and other mature industries could become so intense as to push Washington and Ottawa into further curtailing imports from other suppliers. This highlights a key dilemma associated with a succession of trade agreements with Latin American countries as proposed by President Bush in his "Enterprise for the Americas" initiative.

The United States and Canada may avoid the pressures on industries that would accompany an expanding Western Hemisphere trading zone by limiting imports from other sources and thereby damaging relations with Asian and European countries. Conversely, should the United States and Canada accept the adjustment costs, their political capacity to cope with trade liberalization could be taxed to the point that they are unable to offer countries outside the Western Hemisphere meaningful concessions in GATT. This would effectively shutting down multilateral progress.

Canadian Interests

The trend toward regional blocs, within which the larger trading powers may have more leverage in defining the rules of the game than they have within the GATT, could be a precarious development for smaller countries.

For smaller EC countries, more rapid trade liberalization within the EC than the GATT has not been problematic so far, because EC processes provide better protection to smaller countries than do GATT processes. Also, there are enough small countries in the EC and safeguards in its voting procedures to ensure that the interests of countries such as the Netherlands or Belgium are not sacrificed to serve the interests of Germany or France.

For Canada, the FTA provides many similar benefits in its relationship with the United States. The FTA incorporates into a bilateral agreement the rights and protections afforded each country by the GATT, and it broadens, deepens and more precisely defines those commitments. It provides Canada with a quick dispute settlement for interpreting and enforcing extended GATT rights and obligations.

Overall, without a bilateral agreement between the United States and Mexico, the FTA provides Canada with a counterbalancing arrangement in the event that regional arrangements in Europe and Asia further impede progress in the GATT or reduce the importance of the GATT altogether.

However, the advent of a Mexico-U.S. agreement that excluded Canada, coupled with the increasing inclination of the United States to manage its trading relationship with Japan bilaterally,[4] could easily reduce the importance of both the GATT and the FTA in U.S. trade policy making and reduce the value of the benefits Canada receives from both agreements. In this regard, it is important to remember that Japan and Mexico are the second and third largest U.S. trading partners—the United States would have established bilateral frameworks for the conduct of 45 per cent of its trading relationships. The momentum that resulted from successful negotiations with Mexico could cause the United States to model additional agreements with Latin American countries after its bilateral arrangement with Mexico and further model its relations with the East Asian NICs after its relations with Japan.

As discussed in Chapter 5, the transitional and trade management provisions that could emerge from Mexico-U.S. negotiations could be damaging to Canadian interests. U.S. agreements with Mexico and other Latin American countries would reduce the benefits of preferential access Canadian industries enjoy under the FTA. Mature industries such as furniture, footwear, steel, basic automotive components, and apparel could be particularly hard hit in both the United States and Canada. Only through participation in whatever arrangement emerges between the United States and Mexico can Canada protect its interests.

These perils to Canadian interests might not be much reduced by a parallel Mexico-Canada agreement, and they would be increased if the United States negotiated a series of bilateral agreements with other Latin American countries.

The special status afforded Canada by virtue of its free trade agreement with the United States would make it very difficult for the United States to rebuke Canada if it chooses to be part of a three-way arrangement and if Canadian negotiators are as eager and ambitious as their U.S. and Mexican counterparts in the speed and scope of agreement the latter sought.

This may not be easy for Canada. The United States and Mexico have more at stake in these negotiations and strong incentives to proceed quickly—namely concerns about the resiliency of President Salinas' economic reforms and Mexican political stability if help is not forthcoming soon in the form of increased access to the U.S. market. If Canada is perceived as dragging its feet, it may end up with a separate two-way deal with Mexico or no deal at all.

If Canada were to join in a three-way deal with Mexico, it could seek one fashioned to be GATT consistent and evolving into gradual conformity with the FTA, including tripartite dispute settlement.[5] The framework that emerged could actually strengthen Canada's hand—Canada would not always face the problem of dealing with its larger neighbour on a one-to-one basis.

The Changing Roles of National Governments

It is not difficult to identify trends altering the roles of national governments in the definition of policies affecting international commerce.

In Europe, EC member governments are ceding much sovereignty, or at least some initiative, for a wide range of policy instruments to community-wide mechanisms. Important examples include product standards, government procurement and the regulation of services and the last important vestiges of national import policies—grey-area trade measures. In addition, there are EC programs to improve technological competitiveness. The campaign to gain acceptance for a single EC currency, and to create an institution to manage it, has become the icon of this process.

Similarly, in North America, the continued process of creating a single U.S.-Canadian market through negotiations in areas such as standards, procurement, subsidies and dumping, and competition policy will limit national policy prerogatives. However, as discussed in Chapter 5, the harmonization require-ments of a two-party trade agreement are much less constraining than those present in the 12 member EC. And, without institu-tional mechanism comparable to the EC commission to articulate and enforce bilateral rules, the resulting reassignment of national sovereignties will be much more limited in North America than in Europe.

The effects of additional trade agreements with Latin American countries are less clear. Mexico, for example, being at a lower level of economic and social development, will likely be under considerable pressure to move towards U.S. practices to assure access to the U.S. market. If a free trade agreement with Mexico and successive agreements with other Latin American countries did not include Canada as a full partner, a hub and spoke system could evolve in which Canada's ability to influence U.S. practices would be severely limited. In contrast, if Canada chooses full involvement in U.S. hemispheric initiatives, North American standards of practice could develop. Canada would have a considerable voice in defining them, and Latin American countries would have to adhere gradually to them to ensure full access to the combined U.S.-Canadian market.

Private Initiatives in the Formulation of Trade Policy

In Canada and the United States, perhaps the most significant trends regarding the roles of national governments have been the devolution of some federal economic policy making responsibilities to private interests and subnational governments.

Private interests—firms and industry associations—have always played an important role in the structuring of import regimes. However, as discussed in Chapter 1, the reduction of tariffs and the virtual elimination of statutory quotas for manufactures through the GATT[6] has increased the significance of contingent protection and enhanced the position of the private sector in defining import regimes.

Trade statutes, instead of strictly defining levels of protection, create processes through which private parties may bring suit before quasi-judicial agencies to raise protection. These processes are complicated and costly both for the litigants and society. However, from the narrow prospective of import-threatened industries, they often prove to be more timely, direct and effective than the lobbying processes required to obtain legislative (statutory) or regulatory remedies.[7]

Canadian industry, with the United States absorbing about 75 per cent of its exports, is particularly vulnerable to the U.S. system of contingent protection. The volume of trade cases is very large, often taxing the staffs of the International Trade Commission and the Department of Commerce in the United States. Technical errors and politically inspired peculiarities in agency findings can impose undeserved and burdensome penalties on Canadian firms and other foreign competitors. In a similar vein, Canada is vulnerable to changes in U.S. trade laws that define the system of contingent protection (for example, changes in the definition of countervailable subsidies) and changes in the regulatory environment.

The FTA provides Canada with special status within the U.S. system of contingent protection and within the broader trade policy making apparatus, and does so in ways that acknowledge the importance of private interests in shaping policies. Of course, the same is true for the United States regarding Canadian processes.

The FTA establishes dispute settlement processes to ensure that U.S. and Canadian government agencies apply trade laws fairly and accurately. FTA Chapter 19 permits firms to appeal findings regarding subsidies and dumping before binational dispute settlement panels. FTA Chapter 11, affords Canada (the United States) preferred access to the U.S. (Canadian) market in the event of global safeguard actions.

In two of the early Chapter 19 cases, binational panels remanded back to the U.S. Department of Commerce on technical grounds findings of dumping by Canadian raspberry producers and countervailable subsidies to Canadian steel rail producers. These errors could have resulted in large and damaging countervailing duties against Canadian producers.[8]

Regarding changes in the laws that define the systems of contingent protection, Chapter 19 exempts Canada (the United States) from changes in U.S. (Canadian) dumping and subsidy/countervailing duty laws unless Canada (the United States) is explicitly named—an unlikely occurrence.

Focusing on changes in other statutes or regulations that afford protection, to the extent they violate the GATT or the FTA, they will likely be subject to Chapter 18 review.

As noted above, Chapter 18 may provide some unanticipated benefits. Although the panel reports regarding Canadian landing requirements for West Coast salmon and herring and U.S. size requirements for imported lobster did not immediately settle the disputes at hand, they did result in consultations and mediation among affected private interests in both countries. In such talks, the knowledge that Washington and Ottawa are under real pressure to reach a compromise and take timely action—coupled with the insights offered by binational panel assessments of the GATT and FTA legality of the practices at issue—may prove helpful in persuading private interests in each country to see the necessity for bridging differences and finding nonpredatory solutions to their problems. This should help insulate the private sector in each country from the protective instincts of the other.

Moreover, these kind of benefits may be achieved without national policies precipitating a Chapter 18 panel, consultations or even discussions within the Canada-United States Trade Commission. In shaping national policies that will affect bilateral trade and competitiveness, the ambiguity of potential GATT and FTA consistency coupled with the prospects for a timely challenge under Chapter 18, have the potential to focus the two national governments, and the private sectors that lobby them, to seek complementary, or at least non-conflicting, approaches to industry problems.

Clearly, the processes instigated and ultimate outcomes of the West Coast salmon and herring and East Coast lobster panels indicate that Chapter 18 panel reports may often result in time-consuming government-to-government and industry-to-industry talks, instead of crisp outcomes. Washington and Ottawa may well determine that it is advantageous to be preventative and cooperative in the formulation of policy, and to encourage their private sectors' interests to think along similar lines.

Governments and Multinational Corporations

Turning to the relationships between governments and MNCs, two salient points emerge from Chapters 4 and 5:

- across the full range of industries, access to and command of technology are critical to the competitiveness of firms and the communities dependent on them;
- the costs of precompetitive research and of developing new products and process are rising exponentially, precipitating a variety of corporate alliances to spread costs and broker risks.

The first trend has provoked intense competition among the states, provinces and communities for investment by the most technologically and managerially competent firms. It has also inspired regionally-based pressures on national governments to protect less-capable, though often large and long-established, employers in a variety of industries.

Such activities will continue to incite bilateral frictions, and as argued in Chapter 5, the bilateral effects of subsidies, procurement and managed trade may be best addressed together in FTA negotiations. However, these negotiations must be conducted within the context of assertive state and provincial industrial policies and whatever new relationship emerges between Ottawa and Quebec.

Regarding the rising cost of R & D, the trend towards globalization and alliances raises two interesting sets of issues.

First, MNCs, by establishing R & D and production facilities around the globe and spawning intricate international alliances, are creating entities with ambiguous national identities. Who will regulate them? Globalized MNCs will become increasingly capable of playing one national government off against another. For example, if restrictions on genetic research are too strict in one country, MNCs can take their research to another country.

To the extent they choose to use it, large countries continue to have the considerable leverage of market access, but smaller countries are less well endowed. In Europe, EC-wide policies could prove to be of significant value to smaller countries. For Canada, harmonizing policies affecting corporate activities with the United States could help, and the FTA provides a forum for such discussions. For example, talks on technical standards may provide an opportunity to address these issues as they mature. In this context, Canada could become increasingly dependent on cooperation with the United States to regulate MNCs that operate within its borders, raising all sorts of dilemmas for Canadian politicians. However, it is important to recognize that the FTA is one vehicle Canada can use to address these regulatory issues, if it chooses; the FTA did not create the problem.

Second, pressure persists on Washington to review and increase the scope of its support for generic precompetitive research. New efforts could emerge in one or several of the following areas: advanced materials; semiconductors and advanced computing technologies; opto-electronics; artificial intelligence and other advanced manufacturing technologies; and biotechnology and medical devices. Canada has capabilities and interests in many of these areas. The real question is whether the Bush Administration will actively engage the private sector in defining and co-funding projects.[9]

A more aggressive U.S. innovation policy would have significant implications for Canada and the FTA. An independent Canadian policy could prove ineffective. As discussed in Chapter 5, policy makers may determine Canada's interests would be best served through an exchange of national treatment with the United States for government-financed R & D projects that otherwise excludes foreign companies.

As noted above, the Congress, for example, in proposed legislation governing foreign participation in joint-production ventures, and the U.S. private sector by inviting Canadian firms to participate in the Microelectronics & Computer Technology Corporation, acknowledged a special status for Canada.

The critical point is that the FTA provides the basis for affording Canada special status among foreign countries in U.S. R & D efforts.

Accommodating the States and Provinces

Constraining the use of subsidies and procurement in the competition for plants and jobs would run up against quite assertive state and provincial policies and bureaucracies.

Since the 1970s, several provinces have pursued rather aggressive industrial policies.[10] In the 1980s, the states have sought to fill the void left by the retreat from federal activism under Presidents Reagan and Bush in regional development and export promotion through vehicles such as state-supported venture capital funds, export financing and marketing, R & D and technology transfer programs, and customized job training.[11] Overall, average state industrial development spending tripled from 1982 to 1988.

It is important to recognize that 28 of the state governors are members of the Democratic Party,[12] and their longstanding hold on the nation's statehouses has given rise to more aggressive philosophies about industrial policy than has been fashionable in the Republican Reagan/Bush White House.

In the areas of joint jurisdiction, such as export promotion, where federal dollars shrank and state commitments climbed in the 1980s, federal-state tensions emerged in some instances. State officials became more assertive in collaborative relationships with federal officials.

In Canada, a new constitutional process, which might devolve substantial political and economic authority to Quebec and the other provinces, could have similar consequences. Historically, Quebec has been more inclined to take a proactive posture in promoting industrial and regional development than other provinces and Ottawa. Greater provincial prerogatives in these areas could lead to a ratchetting up of competition among the states and provinces.

Some state and provincial industrial policies are clearly productive. For example, efforts to facilitate technology transfer to smaller firms have the potential to increase national productivity and competitiveness.

Other practices are clearly counterproductive. Locational subsidies—the packages of incentives assembled to attract a new plant to a specific locale—may be the best example. Often state and provincial treasuries engage in competition to attract a plant that would have located in North America in any case. Individual states and provinces cannot forswear the use of such incentives alone, without risking the loss of new plants to other states and provinces. The states cannot forswear location subsidies without the participation of the provinces.

The FTA provides the opportunity for the two national governments to bring together the states and provinces to address locational subsidies but, as always, there are complications.

The Congress

Negotiating disciplines on the counterproductive state and provincial locational subsidies brings to the fore the familiar wild cards in U.S.-Canadian relations—the Congress and the provincial governments.

In Washington, divisions between the Republican Administration and the Democratic Congress with regard to the appropriate scope of federal activities are critical. Since the growth of state activism was in large measure a response to a federal withdrawal from economic development responsibilities engineered by President Reagan, the Democratic Congress may be reluctant to endorse international arrangements which constrain the prerogatives of the states.

Although reasonable people may disagree about the efficacy of many programs, most people, regardless of political stripe can see the counterproductive effects of using locational subsidies in jurisdictional competition for industry. However, the distinction between locational subsidies and more beneficial forms of state aid can become easily blurred in negotiations across the 49th parallel or along Pennsylvania Avenue. In seeking congressional approval for constraints on the state use of locational subsidies, strong support from the statehouses will be necessary.

The Provinces and the Quebec Issue

The failure of the Meech Lake Accord in June 1990 adds new uncertainties. Canada faces a period of intense constitutional debate, and it is difficult to assess the consequences of a new constitutional process for bilateral relations without knowing its parameters.

Nevertheless, it is important to remain firmly focused on the fact that much of the liberalization anticipated from the FTA is to be achieved through follow-on negotiations and the meaning of many provisions of the agreement have to be worked out through consultation and discussion.[13]

Ottawa's commitments in the 1986-88 negotiations represent a rather centrist vision of appropriate national industrial, trade, energy, and foreign investment policies. Undertakings regarding specific actions and future negotiations articulate a middle-of-the-road view about the constraints that may be reasonably placed on Canadian policy prerogatives in exchange for comparable commitments on U.S. actions.

Devolution of economic power to Quebec or all the provinces would likely result in more varied Canadian preferences regarding goals for the evolution of the FTA and the interpretation of its provisions. A more independent Quebec could find some commitments, for example those regarding foreign investment, too confining.[14] Although Quebec strongly favoured free trade with the United States, the FTA might not work as smoothly or evolve as effectively with a more economically autonomous Quebec.

This said, Quebec and the other provinces will continue to have an important stake, and perhaps a greater stake, in access to the U.S. market in a federal structure characterized by more dispersed policy making powers. The desire to sustain free trade could prove to be a centripetal force on provincial policies.

A New Special Relationship

The FTA was an important achievement for both the United States and Canada.

By sweeping away tariffs, limiting non-tariff barriers, establishing binational review of import actions, antidumping and subsidy/countervailing duties, extending GATT protections to business services, and defining the standards of fair treatment for foreign investment, the agreement will provide expanding benefits over the years ahead. As importantly, though, the agreement establishes the means for better managing bilateral relations.

For the United States, the FTA has become part of an alternative or supplemental strategy to multilateral efforts. Should progress in the GATT be slow, it provides the basis for maintaining stability and continuing progress with its largest trading partner. As significantly, the FTA may become part of a continental or even hemispheric strategy as the United States and Canada seek a free trade agreement with Mexico and to encourage liberal trade and investment policies throughout Latin America.

For Canada, the task of managing its international and domestic economic policies has always been strongly influenced by the prospects for its resource exports, the constraints imposed by technology and market size on its manufacturers, and the trade and industrial policies of its principal trading partner. With regard to the latter, there has been much change and there continues to be considerable uncertainty.

The FTA re-establishes the special relationship by creating processes to resolve issues and a context for seeking new avenues of cooperation as both countries respond to changes in the international environment.

For example, as the United States negotiates with Mexico, undertakes broader hemispheric trade initiatives or perhaps adopts more aggressive industrial policies in high-technology areas, frequently Canadians may determine that their preferred long-term policy path is not to insulate themselves from U.S. actions. Rather, their best option may be to engage the Americans in a partnership, for example, to help define the rules for expanding hemispheric trade or to build more competitive continental enterprises.

For Canada and its political leaders, so engaging the United States can involve significant short-term economic and political costs. This is why the immediate commercial benefits created by improved market access under the FTA are much more important than simple cost-benefit analyses would reveal. In many ways, the more immediate benefits that flow from liberalized trade and investment are the glue that holds the FTA together in the short run. The most significant long-term benefits from free-trade likely will be the processes and new context for managing Canadian-U.S. relations established under the Free Trade Agreement.

The trade agreement gives Canada a check on U.S. actions enjoyed by no other country. It subjects careless or politically-coloured U.S. actions to rigourous binational scrutiny. This said, the agreement does much more—it re-establishes Canada's claim to a special consideration in the U.S. policy-making apparatus. As the U.S. assesses the outcome of the Uruguay Round and negotiates with Mexico, this may prove to be the most important free trade agreement benefit of all for Canada.

The U.S. wants to conclude a trade deal with Mexico quickly for political reasons, and Canada's presence at the negotiating table only complicates matters. Dealing alone, the Americans could shape rules-of-origin, safeguards and other mechanisms to cushion the adjustments in the U.S. in ways that are damaging to Canadian interests. But in the atmosphere of cooperation fostered by the agreement, the U.S. is hard pressed to deal Canada out if Canada recognizes the American sense of urgency. And so it would be in talks with Chile, Brazil and other Latin players.

In the decade ahead, no country has a greater stake in influencing U.S. policy than Canada. By providing a forum for negotiations on a whole range of industrial policies from agriculture to transportation, and creating a new spirit of bilateral cooperation, the free trade agreement provides Canada with the means to defend its national interests.

Notes

1. Large multinational corporations engaged in secondary manufacturing have more options to choose from in seeking to hedge against the risks contingent protection imposes.

2. Similar observations apply to the informal, Japan-centred trading bloc emerging in Asia.

3. Even should Canada reverse course and decide not to participate in a trade agreement between the United States and Mexico, the adjustments imposed on Canadian industry would be substantial, owing to its reliance on the U.S. market.

4. Through, for example, the Structural Impediments Initiatives talks and agreements.

5. Michael Hart has suggested that the FTA be extended to include Mexico—his assessment is that the problems of accommodating Mexico's particular aspirations and circumstances are manageable. Michael Hart, *A North American Free Trade Agreement: The Strategic Implications for Canada* (Ottawa: Centre for Trade Policy and Law and The Institute for Research on Public Policy, 1990).

6. Generally, the GATT prohibits the use of quotas to control trade on industrial products. It permits temporary quotas as part of emergency balance of payments programs and as part of escape clause (safeguard) actions.

7. This said, the private sectors in both countries often can be quite effective in achieving statutory and regulatory protection when the system of contingent protection does not offer a remedy. In 1989, the success of U.S. fishermen in obtaining legislation that raised minimum size requirements for imported Canadian lobster provides one example.

8. See The Bureau of National Affairs Inc., *International Trade Reporter*, (Washington, D.C.: May 9, 1990), pp. 660-661; (May 16, 1990), 691; and (July 18, 1990), pp. 1101-1102.

9. It is worth noting that the EC and Japan each devote about 4 per cent of their R & D spending to consortium projects with about 50 per cent of the funding provided by the public sectors. For the

United States the comparable figures are less than 1 and 20 per cent. Department of Commerce, *Emerging Technologies*, (Spring 1990), pp. 49.

10. For a review, for example, of Ontario and Quebec policies see Morici, Smith and Lea, *Canadian Industrial Policy*, Chapter 6.

11. DeWitt John, *Shifting Responsibilities* (Washington, D.C.: National Governors' Association, 1987), p. 1.

12. As of February 1, 1991, 28 were Democrats, 19 were Republicans, 2 were Independents and 1 seat (Arizona) was in dispute.

13. For example, regarding investment performance requirements, Canadian policy makers readily concede that Chapter 16 of the FTA constrains them not to impose trade-related foreign investment performance requirements (e.g., import substitution, domestic content or export goals). However, they argue that non-trade-related requirements (e.g., R & D spending goals, technology transfer and job training) are legitimized, because they are not specifically prohibited by the agreement. U.S. officials do not share this view, especially as they relate to R & D and technology. Some officials want future negotiations to address this issue.

14. It might, for example, wish to be more assertive than the Canadian position regarding R & D-related performance for foreign-investors.

Appendix

Table A-1
Price Indices for Canada's Commodity Exports and for All Industrial Products and GDP
(1981=100)

	Wheat	Other Farm and Fish	Crude Petroleum	Natural Gas	Metals and Minerals	Forest Prod.	Chemicals and Fertilizer	All Industrial Prod.	GDP Deflator	Import Prices
1981	100.0	100.0	100.0	100.0	100.0	100.0	100.0	100.0	100.0	100.0
1982	92.5	100.3	84.2	106.0	91.0	97.0	99.3	106.7	108.7	104.3
1983	91.0	97.0	77.5	96.9	92.7	95.4	96.6	110.4	114.1	103.7
1984	93.2	102.8	79.8	90.3	93.1	101.6	99.9	115.4	117.1	109.6
1985	93.5	103.2	80.9	75.4	92.0	109.0	98.8	118.6	120.7	113.4
1986	76.5	100.6	42.4	58.2	94.8	112.1	92.3	119.6	123.6	112.8
1987	62.2	103.9	51.3	44.9	95.4	125.4	97.4	122.8	129.0	112.2
1988	91.0	108.4	37.2	40.3	97.4	130.4	106.1	128.0	134.3	110.5

Source: *Bank of Canada Review* (July, 1989).

Table A-2
The Distribution of U.S. Imports from Mexico and Canada
(Per cent)

		Mexico		Canada	
		1979 %	1987 %	1979 %	1987 %
SITC					
0	Food and Live Animals	16.6	10.2	3.5	4.3
1	Beverages and Tobacco	0.9	1.4	0.9	0.7
2	Crude Materials, Inedible, Except Minerals	3.1	1.9	15.9	9.4
3	Mineral Fuels, Lubricants, and Related Products	35.2	19.4	14.3	9.6
32	Coal, Coke, and Briquettes	*	*	0.1	0.1
33	Petroleum and Related Products	35.1	19.1	6.5	6.4
34	Gas, Natural and Manufactured	0.1	0.3	7.6	3.1
4	Animal and Vegetable Oils, Fats, Waxes	*	*	*	0.1
5	Chemicals and Related Products, NES	2.2	2.0	6.4	4.3
51	Organic Chemicals	0.3	0.3	1.3	0.7
52	Inorganic Chemicals	1.4	0.7	2.3	1.5
53	Dyeing, Tanning, Colouring Materials	*	0.1	*	0.1
54	Medicinal, Pharmaceutical Products	0.1	0.1	0.1	0.1
55	Essential Oils, Perfumes, Soaps, Cleansers	0.2	0.2	0.1	0.1
56	Fertilizers, Manufactured	*	*	2.2	0.9
57	Explosives, Pyrotechnic Products	*	*	0.1	*
58	Artificial Resins and Plastics, Ethers	*	0.6	0.2	0.6
59	Chemical Materials and Products	0.1	0.1	0.2	0.2
6	Manufactured Goods Classified by Mat.	9.9	10.2	19.0	19.0
61	Leather and Furskins	0.2	0.3	0.1	0.1
62	Rubber Manufactures	0.1	0.3	0.8	0.9
63	Cord and Wood Manufactures	1.0	0.6	1.0	0.9
64	Paper, Paperboard, Articles of Pulp	0.6	1.4	7.5	7.4
65	Textile Yarns, Fabrics, NES	0.7	0.9	0.1	0.5
66	Non-Metallic Mineral Manufactures, NES	1.2	2.0	1.0	1.0
67	Iron and Steel	0.8	1.1	2.5	2.2
68	Non-Ferrous Metals	4.2	2.3	4.3	4.0
69	Manufactures of Metals	1.1	1.4	1.8	1.9

		Mexico		Canada	
		1979 %	*1987* %	*1979* %	*1987* %
7	Machinery and Transport Equipment	21.0	42.6	34.2	43.4
71	Power Gen. Machinery and Equipment	1.6	5.9	2.8	3.3
72	Machinery Specific by Industry	0.6	0.4	2.8	2.0
73	Metalworking Machinery	0.1	*	0.3	0.2
74	Industrial Machinery and Equip., NES	0.6	2.0	1.8	1.7
75	Office Machines and Data Processors	0.8	2.3	1.0	1.7
76	Telecommunications	7.5	8.5	0.8	0.9
77	Electrical Machinery and Parts	7.3	13.9	1.4	2.6
78	Road Vehicles	2.1	9.4	21.9	29.0
79	Other Transportation Equipment	0.5	0.1	1.5	2.0
8	Misc. Manufactured Articles	7.9	8.6	2.7	4.8
81	Plumbing, Heating, Lighting Fixtures	0.2	0.3	*	*
82	Furniture and Parts Thereof	0.4	1.5	0.9	1.5
83	Travel Goods, Handbags	0.3	0.1	*	*
84	Articles of Apparel, Clothing Accessories	2.5	2.1	0.1	0.4
85	Footwear	0.5	0.5	0.1	0.1
87	Scientific, Controlling Instruments	0.6	1.4	0.3	0.7
88	Photographic Equip., Watches, Clocks	0.2	0.2	0.2	0.3
89	Misc. Manufactured Articles, NES	3.1	2.4	1.1	1.9
9	Commodities and Transactions, NES	3.2	3.7	3.1	4.4
	Total in millions of U.S. Dollars	8,994.1	20,511.2	38,459.8	70,644.1

* = less than 0.05 per cent

Source: Organization for Economic Cooperation and Development, *Foreign Trade by Commodities: Series C.*

Other Joint Centre-Institute Publications

Order address:
The Institute for Research on Public Policy
P.O. Box 3670 South
Halifax, Nova Scotia
B3J 3K6
1-800-565-0659 (toll free)

Related Institute Publications

Order address:
The Institute for Research on Public Policy
P.O. Box 3670 South
Halifax, Nova Scotia B3J 3K6
1-800-565-0659 (toll free)